STALKING TROUT
A SERIOUS FISHERMAN'S GUIDE

STALKING TROUT
A SERIOUS FISHERMAN'S GUIDE

By
Les Hill & Graeme Marshall

SeTo Publishing

The
Halcyon
Press

Published jointly by

The Halcyon Press
C.P.O. Box 360, Auckland, 1
&
SeTo Publishing
C.P.O. Box 4028, Auckland, 1

First published 1985

©Les Hill and Graeme Marshall

All photographs by
Les Hill and Graeme Marshall
Illustrations by
Grant Winter

ISBN 0-908697-04-X

Design: Halcyon Press
Layout & Finished Art: Stu Duval
Production: Selwyn Jacobson
Typesetting: Jacobsons Graphic Communications Group
Printed in Hong Kong through Colorcraft Limited.

North American Edition by
Stone Wall Press, Inc.
1241 30th Street NW
Washington, DC 20007
ISBN 0-913276-51-0

CONTENTS

Preface for North American Fishermen

New Zealand has long been considered the "Mecca" for North American trout fishermen. Somehow, while our fishing gets worse, theirs just gets better and better. Most of us plan and save for that dream trip for years. In New Zealand the streams are crystal clear and the trout are huge — and **very** wily.

If you can "stalk" monster trout successfully in New Zealand, imagine how it will enhance your results on famous North American trout waters such as the Battenkill, Madison and Au Sable — heavily fished waters — as well as your favorite stream.

Though this book is written by Kiwis for Kiwis, certain aspects of fishing are the same the world over. We believe that the techniques of stalking trout are as pertinent to North America as they are "Down Under". And while you will have to put up with metric units, New Zealand colour (sic), humor and argot, you'll also get a lot of local insider fishing information. If you're headed "Down Under", this can't help but be useful. If not . . . well, you can dream. Have a look at the magnificent color photo sequence after page 64 — and drool.

We're making this book available to you intact. Hopefully it will add another dimension to your successful trout fishing experience and provide a good read. We further hope you enjoy the extra touches (including the photographs, cartoons, and nifty drawings) as much as we do.

Tight Lines,

Stone Wall Press

Authors Note

The contents and spirit of this book have emerged from one word — why? The reason is simple — the word encourages, asks for understanding. Only from understanding can progress, development and refinement evolve. Such was our aim — to better our angling, and in so doing record it and pass on our findings.

From time to time we have fished with a great many anglers, and in observing them and ourselves in success we came to the conclusion that the one skill paramount in assuring regular good fortune was the ability to spot trout. An angler who possessed that ability seldom knew failure. This did *not* mean a limit bag on each outing, but at least one fish. From this point other ideas snowballed. The obvious question was, why did some anglers spot more fish? We concluded that it was because they knew what to look for and where to look. They understood, too, that their conduct on a river ensured their success. They had some knowledge of a trout's senses and used its weaknesses to their advantage during the ultimate act of capture. In addition, the best anglers have a real empathy for their sport and all that goes with it — the companionship, the dreams, the environment.

We try in this book to convey to our readers some of our thoughts, observations and opinions. These are based on years of contemplation and practice, expressed often as generalisations. In so stating, we could, equally, quote numerous contradictions — such is the beauty and character of fishing! Such, too, is the fickle nature of trout. Statements about trout and trout fishing cannot be unequivocal — we hope ours are not read that way.

While writing this book we were separated by 960 kilometres. I lived in Invercargill and Graeme in Nelson. Consequently we had literally hundreds of kilometres and hosts of rivers of widely different character to observe. This assisted us immeasurably in our research. Communication had some obvious difficulties so we elected to take individual responsibility for specific chapters and to write these predominantly in the first person. Chapters 1, 2, 3, 4, 9, and half of 8 were my contribution, while Graeme wrote chapters 5, 6, 7, and half of 8.

Finally, we hope that what we have presented adds something to angling literature in New Zealand, and is of benefit to beginners and seasoned anglers alike.

Les Hill

Introduction

Mention excitement, endless concentration, acute alertness and strenuous exercise, and few would consider you were speaking about fishing. These descriptions are reserved, in most minds, for spectacular sports like mountaineering or hang gliding. To some, though, they accurately describe trout fishing — they portray the fine art of stalking trout.

Man, since his beginning, has been instinctively drawn to (and has survived by!) hunting. Stalking trout is hunting in every sense. Man's quarry, the trout, has developed refined powers for survival. It has evolved excellent camouflage and ever alert senses — not to mention a fickle nature. To succeed, an angler not only has to pit himself against these skills, but better them. He must concentrate on how he steps, his deportment, his speed — in other words his own camouflage. In addition, he must be alert for every little hint of a trout — usually he will be granted little more! Every niche, every shape, shadow or movement must be considered. The quarry has to be detected without its knowledge of ensuing danger. The stalk is exciting enough in itself, but forms only the foundation of the total act. Trembling hands testify anticipation of victory as the trout is lured. Fooled or not, there is always the next one — then the next. Hours, days pass unnoticed, the world forgotten. The enticement of 'what may be around the next bend' draws an angler for miles, up banks, along rocky reaches, through scrub and trees. Distance disappears, unnoticed, until the return journey is undertaken.

To many people, fishing is viewed as an ideal pastime for the elderly. Among the virtues of the sport are the peace and tranquility of the riverside and the slow, untroubled yet thoughtful pace of the day. Ask many people to describe a day's fishing and they will conjure up a picture of a rod propped up on a forked stick. The fisherman is described as a harmless soul who lies back in the nearby shade with seemingly endless patience. Through his mind flow images of previously successful afternoons, or maybe he contemplates the possibilities of the opposite bank. To others, fishing is casting a threadline lure far out into a pool and retrieving it through its promising depths. Large, deep pools, tantalising and mysterious, suggest the possibility of large fish lying deep. This lure can occupy the angler for hours. The fly fisherman is considered the most thoughtful artist on the river. His casting is effortless and his passage along the river bank slow and deliberate. He can sit motionless for hours waiting for a mayfly hatch and the onset of a rise. Even then he exercises extreme care in selecting a fly and takes his time in tying it onto his line before creeping into position ready for action.

These portraits accurately describe fishing for most, and long may they be re-enacted. But, as in most pursuits, there are new horizons and pinnacles for the adventurous. Stalking trout offers these and more to a fisherman. Stalking trout is exciting, effective. Perhaps the ultimate fishing experience!

1

The Senses

Like a good wine, one's patience and perseverance improve with age. I can remember days on the river with my father when I was about eleven years of age. Such periods of sustained action are easily recalled but so, too, are the many times when no sign of trout was evident. On these occasions my father would continue fishing, but I had not learned the value of patience. Other riverside attractions would soon distract my energies.

Invariably my enthusiasm would be rekindled immediately my father hooked a fish. This reassurance that there were trout to be caught would spring me back into more positive action.

Similarly, if I was losing heart while still fishing and an unwary trout struck — then the excitement would rise dramatically and casting become more purposefully directed, and reflexes more acutely tuned!

It was the knowledge of the trout's presence and reassurance of a willingness to take which had to be continually rekindled.

I now find that with a little experience of where to go and the confidence and ability to 'spot' a percentage of feeding trout, this high level of excitement is maintained all the time I fish. The essential factor, of course, is to spot before being spotted. Nothing will improve this skill more than hours (or more accurately, years) of practice.

There are, however, precautions one can take to reduce the chances of being detected by the ever wary and alert trout — an understanding, for example, of trout's senses, and their vision in particular.

A fish's eye is very similar to its human counterpart. The light receptor cells are of two types. *Cone cells* are the colour receptors while *rod cells* are very sensitive in detecting light intensity.

The fish's eye is round, and focussing cannot be affected by changing the eye shape. Short-sightedness is a result of the round lens although focussing on distant objects is possible as retractor muscles can move the lens backwards.

The brown trout has excellent powers of lens movement with strong retractor muscles. Trout have an egg shaped lens with the pointed end facing the retina. There is some ability in trout to focus on near and far objects at the same time because of this shape. Among many other

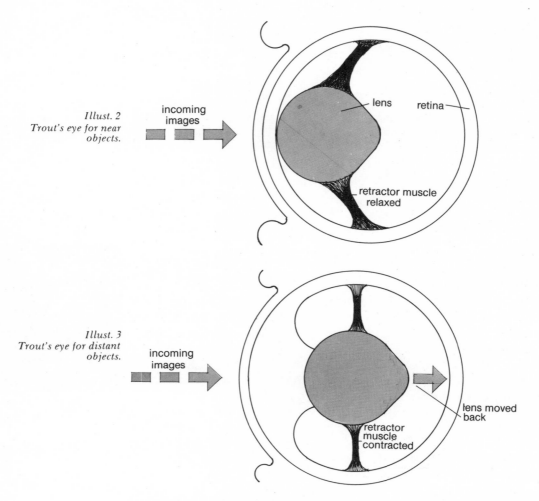

*Illust. 2
Trout's eye for near
objects.*

incoming
images

lens   retina

retractor muscle
relaxed

*Illust. 3
Trout's eye for distant
objects.*

incoming
images

lens moved
back

retractor
muscle
contracted

subjects, fishermen often argue about a trout's ability to see *colour*. The simple answer is that they do.

The presence of cone cells (colour receptors) provides initial evidence which is strengthened by colour-absorbing pigments contained inside the cells.

Sherwood E. Peterson noted positive responses to coloured lights during an experiment he conducted. He showed that the behaviour of brook, brown and rainbow trout could be conditioned with coloured lights.

Many believe that colours are clearer to the trout under water rather than above. This is probably true, but do not underestimate the fish's ability to detect unnatural shades on the bank. Until recently I have been careful to wear clothing matching the colours of my surroundings when stalking trout. A waterproof and comparatively inexpensive coat was offered to me. Sensing a bargain I accepted, remembering many days with water dripping down my neck or seeping through at the elbows and shoulders. The only drawback with the garment was its bright red colour. I have worn the coat only twice while pursuing my favourite foe. On both occasions I remained dry but was amazed at how easily I was seen by the fish.

This experience adds weight to the argument that trout are very sensitive to shades in the red end of the spectrum.

During my fishing days I have observed many responses by trout, apparently to changes and variations in colour. I remember one balmy day on the lower Mataura. Several trout fed in the edge of a gentle ripply run. I flicked a Greenwell's Light up to the first. It looked, but declined. A hasty change to Greenwell's Dark was more successful. The two flies were identical in all respects except the colour.

Another time I fished The Travers in Nelson. A friend had asked me to try out a newly created dry fly. He had tied me six — all were similar except that two had a red tinge not unlike that of a Red Tipped Governor. The trout demonstrated an unrelenting preference for the red ones.

Hunters all demonstrate a common behaviour in that they are religiously cautious. The deer stalker, for example, endeavours to avoid

Hunters are aware their game is sensitive to scent.

making even the slightest noise or displaying obvious movement but more importantly is keenly aware of the wind direction and where it is carrying his scent. This trait shows an understanding of the senses of the prey. This knowledge is acquired for the obvious reason that it adds to success.

An understanding of some of the trout's senses would similarly assist a fisherman.

While waiting in hope of an early afternoon rise on the Upper Mataura, a friend and I sorted and discussed flies. "What size is this one?" asked my less experienced companion.

"An 18," I said. But further investigation soon showed that I was wrong — it was a 16. Side by side the two were difficult to differentiate, so my mistake was somewhat understandable. The frailty of human senses was soon to be emphasized even more.

The onset of a Mataura rise can be a spontaneous affair. It was this day. One moment a smooth glassy pool, then dimples everywhere. Knowing that a hatch may only last a short time, we sprang into action — each going in different directions. A quick inspection of a drifting mayfly showed it had a distinct quill body, so I hastily chose a size 16 (I think!) Dad's Favourite and attached it to my leader. Wading into the river in the tail of a long pool I eased in behind a good fish — a 'sitter' I mused. With no obstructions, casting was easy — or was it? Nervous tension cramped the style. Anyway, my fly found its way to the fish's feeding line and up he came, confident and hungry. Obviously he was more discerning than anticipated — my fly was refused.

A quick change of pattern renewed my confidence. "This time," I thought. The trout thought otherwise. Again he rose to inspect. It was not to his liking. I had read in the past, and been told, that if the fish was very selective it was often more profitable to change to a smaller fly rather than to a new pattern. Worth a try. Close inspection convinced me that my new offering was smaller — an 18. The initial response from the fish was the same, but this time his apparent confidence was indicated by sipping my fly from sight.

The hatch lasted for over an hour. During that time I hooked five fish. Three of them inspected but refused a size 16 fly, but took an 18 in the same pattern. Their eyesight, it seemed, was at least the equal of mine. *Trout are extremely sensitive to movement.* Stationary objects often remain unobserved while movement probably suggests one of two things — danger or food.

One situation which demonstrates the trout's acute vision and ability to detect movement is fishing in the shallows of a high country lake. One such lake was actually part of a river system which had been dammed by earthquake debris. The edges harboured many cruising trout patrolling a territorial 'beat' which could soon be mapped. A trout was chosen as the victim. Dry flies left floating in the foraging fish's path were refused, so my fishing companion, Graeme Marshall, took an ever faithful size 16 Pheasant Tail Nymph from his box. When the trout had passed on his run and was out of sight the nymph was cast delicately onto the water and allowed to sink slowly to the muddy lake bed. Like clockwork the trout reappeared on his usual path and started in the direction of the fly.

Graeme and I share the same nervous tension when there is a fish ever in sight. Our disposition at this time was to keep as low as possible yet continue to observe that most exciting instant for any fisherman — the moment of the take! We dared move only our eyes. The speckled Wild Brown drew nearer and nearer the place where the nymph should lie, then crossed the stationary nylon tippet and continued past. We could not see the nymph so we guessed that maybe the trout couldn't either. Graeme therefore gently took the floating line in one hand and again we waited. The trout was soon in sight and easing towards the nymph. This time, when it was about two metres from the offering, Graeme gently tugged the line, lifting the tiny Pheasant Tail daintily off the mud. There was an immediate response from the trout. Not a violent change but a slight turn and a barely noticeable acceleration. The white of the inside of the mouth showed as the nymph was taken.

Sighting such a minute bait, especially when moved so imperceptively, tells much about the trout's awareness of movement.

While motions in the water can frequently signify the presence of food to a trout *action outside must often imply danger*. Again, a practical situation can demonstrate the truth in this.

My favourite fishing is in isolated waters where peace and solitude equal the attraction of the fishing quality. I recall setting out one sunny summer morning to such a place. The sun was filtering down through a misty atmosphere created by the damp Westland bush.

A freely moving figure was soon sighted in the eye of a sunlit pool. In unfrequented places we can easily be deceived into the misconception that a feeding trout is easy quarry. I was on this occasion. After two false casts I put the line onto the water. I did not see the fish disappear but was soon aware that the moving shape had gone. The fact that a shooting line had spooked the trout taught me two lessons. The first was that movement will often signify danger to a trout and stop its feeding. The second, that we must always remember shadow length, early and late during the day in question, and watch our position, or the position of our line, with respect to the angle of the sun.

In his book, 'Nymphs and the Trout', Frank Sawyer similarly observes the danger of a line shadow. 'It is of course true that animals and fish, and indeed ourselves, have difficulty discerning movement while looking towards the sun, and an angler approaching a fish with the sun behind him is much less likely to be seen that one from the opposite angle. But in fishing it is not solely the angler or his movements which cause the alarm, rather far more often the shadow of the line and the cast as it falls to the water, and this is what the fisherman must keep foremost in his mind.'

Having established that trout are very sensitive to movement, can distinguish colour and have some ability for near and far sight, there are a number of light factors which affect the fish's vision and hence the approach by a stalking angler. First, light rays striking the water surface at less than 10° are reflected. Because rays reaching the surface at less than 10° are reflected *a trout's vision above the surface or outside the water is restricted*. The closer a fish is to the surface the greater the restriction, or conversely the deeper a fish lies then the wider its view of the outside. Light rays reaching the water surface at an angle greater than 10° penetrate the water and are refracted (bent) downwards.

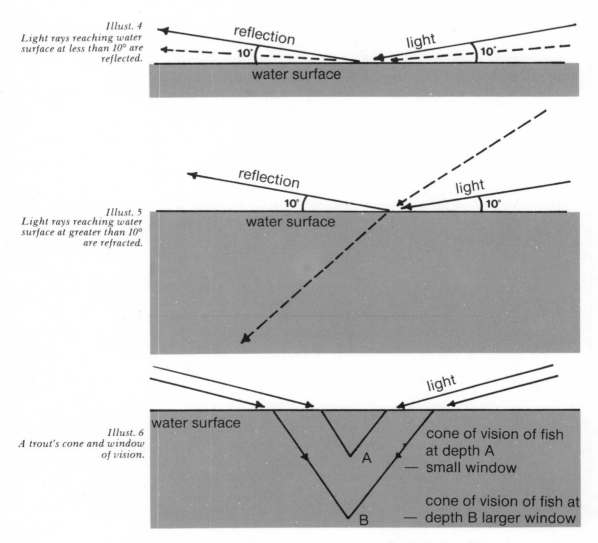

Illust. 4
Light rays reaching water surface at less than 10° are reflected.

reflection · light · 10° · 10° · water surface

Illust. 5
Light rays reaching water surface at greater than 10° are refracted.

reflection · light · 10° · 10° · water surface

Illust. 6
A trout's cone and window of vision.

light · water surface · A · cone of vision of fish at depth A — small window · B · cone of vision of fish at depth B larger window

*Our quarry and his senses — 'Fly Fishing For Trout" Carl Massey — 'A fish 1.2 m deep would have a window over 2.4 m in diameter in a complete circle above his head. When the fish comes up to within 30 cm of the surface, his window would be only about 60 cm in diameter.'

Trout's eyes are placed laterally on the head and are tilted forward and upward. *Vision is therefore restricted downward and to the rear. A blind spot is thus created behind a fish* — about 35° on either side. High objects to the rear are still in sight.

Given a calm water surface, if the angler and his rod are not more than 1.5 m above the surface of the water, they would be invisible to the fish at approximately 9 m. (Do not forget that this is 1.5 m above the water surface, not ground level.) At a distance of 12 m the fisherman could stand to a height of 2 m and at 15 m, to a height of 2.5 m.

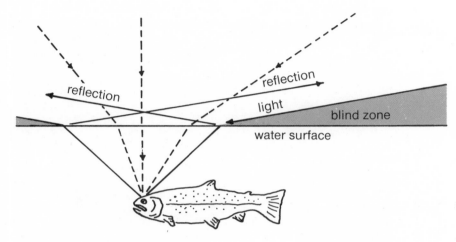

Illust. 7
A trout's view outside the water.

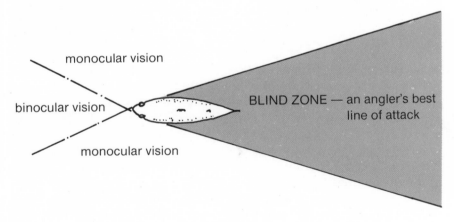

Illust. 8
A trout's range of sight.

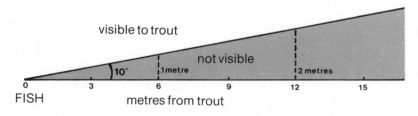

Illust. 9
Zones of visibility and invisibility for a trout.

17

Sound

Fish have a well developed sense of hearing — not surprising given that sound moves five times faster through water than through air. A wide range of sound frequencies can be perceived through the use of *two detection systems*.

On either side of the head ears are buried, in a similar position to the

inner ears of human beings. There is no duct to the outside so sound waves are transmitted directly through the skin, bone and flesh.

Along both sides of a trout's body is a distinct line which is easily seen. This shows the presence of the *lateral line* which is the second sound detector.

The lateral line is a network of canals which are all interconnected. The canals contain sensor cells called neuromasts. Sound waves pass through openings on the lateral line to pairs on the neuromasts. Nerve fibres continue the passage of a signal to the brain.

Water molecules are affected by two different sounds. *Near Field Sounds* emanate with pressure waves that force the molecules to vibrate back and forth without being displaced.

The lateral line system detects the near field sounds or those of low frequency (10 cycles per second to 200 cps) while the ears concentrate on the far field ones. The two systems therefore complement each other.

One further consideration of sound detection is the reflectivity of the water surface. 99.9% of sound energy in the *air* is reflected so *normal talking is not perceptible* to fish. An extreme test demonstrating this point was conveyed by Carl Massey who wrote, "I can well remember a test carried out by my father on the Goodradigbee River over fifty years ago

Most sound energy in air is reflected by surface of water.

GRANT WINTER

when he fired both barrels of a shotgun into the air, close to a trout, and this had no apparent effect on the fish.'' Despite being aware of such stories I still instinctively reduce my voice when a large fish is feeding close!

I would like to stress the difference between the two outside mediums of air and ground. The ground we walk on is an extension of the river bed *so vibrations caused on the bank are easily transmitted to the fish.*

A stalking fisherman must continually remind himself of the need to tread softly when walking along a bank or not to knock rocks together when wading. This lesson was re-taught to a fishing friend, Dave Lyttle, very recently as we enjoyed a weekend on the Maruia River.

Dave's keen eye caught the splendid sight of a large brown shape dimpling the water surface frequently. We were sneaking along a high bank thick with native beech at the time, so I lay on my belly to remain completely out of sight while retaining the luxury of an unobstructed view of the battle to come. Dave retreated downstream then carefully began climbing down the steep bank. There was no chance of the trout seeing him as he was obscured by a thick cover of bush.

Vibrations on bank or river bed travel quickly and easily to trout.

I am not sure which I heard first, the rock or the curses. Dave had loosened, then dislodged, a sizeable stone which bounced down the bank and stopped against a stump a metre from the water's edge.

"Fish still there?" yelled Dave.

"Yes," was my reply. But, no sooner had the word been uttered when the trout began drifting slowly downstream, sinking deeper and deeper as it went.

Yet another trout had retained its freedom because of acute senses which are ever tuned and alert.

A CURRENT TRICK

SOMETIMES WE ARE LUCKY enough to hook a large trout or salmon on our fly rod, only to have the fish get below us in the strong river current.

When this happens, I put the tip of my rod down into the water and apply pressure slowly. The change of the angle of pull against the fish often causes it to swim back upstream.

By pumping the rod and taking up the small amount of line gained each time, I can usually make the catch swim back upstream a considerable distance in a heavy current. This trick has saved many a fine catch for me.

—HOWARD E. MOODY

POINT THE ROD TIP DOWN INTO WATER.

...TO TURN THE FISH UPSTREAM

$F\xi \cdot$ 12/65

A similar incident illustrating the same point was the result of a very elementary error on my part. I was casting to a nymphing fish with a size 12 March Brown. Curiosity was shown but the nymph was not taken so I resolved to change to a size 14 of the same pattern. The solitary one I had in my fly box possessed a hook which was slightly straightened so I bent down and picked up a stone. Pushing the hook point against the stone solved the problem. Rather than replacing the rock gently into the water, at my feet, I lobbed it onto the bank where it bounced off a large boulder. The response from the trout was immediate and rapid.

Try putting your head under water sometime and get someone to bang two stones together or hit a rock on the river bed nearby. Understanding the above response will be apparent.

Smell

As the stalking fisherman is generally walking upstream where there is a relatively swift current his scent would rarely reach the trout. For this reason the sense of smell is of lesser importance here but would be outlined in more detail if we were dealing with discrimination of food.

However, on occasions, such as crossing a stream before fishing at its junction, crossing a river upstream of a fish, fishing downstream, or casting in a backcurrent, we do offer a chance of our odour being conveyed. It is therefore essential that we are aware that fish can sense a far greater range of odour-producing chemicals in the water than we can in the air.

While stalking one side of a river we often, from an elevated position, spot trout on the attractive opposite bank. Not so bad on a small stream, but frustrating on less fordable rivers. Graeme Marshall and I met this situation while stalking the Motupiko Stream in a very low flow. From a patch of bush we watched a trout nymphing opposite. Graeme could not resist the temptation. An upstream crossing offered the best access to the fish and was undoubtedly beyond the fish's vision. I waited in the bush to act as a guide. Graeme stealthily made his way up to the next rapid and was soon through the knee-deep water and circling wide of the fish. The fish fed on undisturbed. Then, maybe a minute after Graeme had crossed, the feeding ceased and I watched the fish fade from view and disappear. We are convinced that Graeme was not sighted, His footfalls were deliberate and careful. The only plausible explanation was smell. The time lapse suggests the same.

Whatever the alert was for this fish, it was a subtle one. But that is what we must be aware of — trout's senses are finely tuned. They have to be to ensure their survival. Your knowledge of this and of how they are tuned can and should benefit your stalking.

2

Where To Look

An empty sports stadium is a spiritless and lonely arena; its character will gradually change as it fills with spectators anticipating an exciting contest.

Rivers and streams can at times appear similarly lifeless. Few will portray this deception as convincingly as the changeable Mataura.

Usually on a clear, calm day numerous fish would search hungrily for hatching insects or drifting nymphs but on one particular afternoon, in perfect conditions, I could have sworn that the trout were elsewhere. This apparent total disappearance of the river's vast stock lasted for several hours, through until sunset.

The sight I then witnessed is notoriously typical, but only fully comprehended by those fortunate enough to have experienced it. It is an event of total transformation, a little bewildering and unbelievable even to an experienced fisherman.

The 'Mad Mataura Rise' or 'Boil' began at first with a few inconspicuous dimples demonstrating that there *were* some fish in the river after all. Three or four ripples multiplied surprisingly to several dozen, which was extraordinary enough considering the earlier inactivity, but still more and more fish joined in the feeding until the surface of the river literally boiled, as hungry trout rose freely from one bank to the other in front of me, behind me, and even right beside me! Some were a mere rod length away!

As the feeding frenzy increased so, too, did my anticipation of inevitable sport but I soon saw a beautiful dream transformed into an incomprehensible nightmare. The very selective feeders were totally oblivious to my offerings despite their changing colour, shape and size.

My suggestion, therefore, is that those of our rivers and streams which maintain a reasonable flow throughout the year probably hold more fish than a superficial survey would suggest. The majority of these fish will reside in the depths of pools and feed on the river bed, perhaps at night, unnoticed by some. These night feeders and bottom dwellers are sought and taken by many anglers. Their prizes are sometimes large, larger than one might expect in the waters I am about to discuss. Their methods are beyond the realms of my discussion since my sole aim is to focus attention on one section of the trout population — that

Photo 4
Happy angler with two
from shallow water.

portion which can be observed feeding during the day — the edge and surface feeders, the 'eye' dwellers. In general terms, the trout foraging in a place out of strong currents.

It is a common belief that the best fishing occurs in the early morning, or in the evening when hatching insects abound, and trout consume their share as they are made available. I will not dispute the marvellous sport there is to be had at these times, but suggest that the middle part of the day holds equal excitement — perhaps not in numbers but certainly in fishing quality. In every river or stream there is always a feeding trout to be found. The secret, of course, is to know where to look.

During a fish's life, its needs for survival are simple and governed by exacting laws of nature. It requires an abundant food supply, and in acquiring this diet it must instinctively maintain contact with safety. Its energy expenditure must not exceed the intake, thus the feeding position in flowing waters is carefully selected (or, in fact, is not selected by the trout but is predetermined by the hydrological nature of the river).

In their passage downstream, rivers know many faces — from waterfalls and cascades to deep, deceptive pools or wide stony shallows; from deep narrow ravines to wide meandering flood plains. Within this changing passage the niches which trout occupy are similarly endless. But, as in many intricate systems, generalisations may be made which aid understanding and allow a reader to expand ideas to suit his experience.

Photo 5
Confluence of stream
and main river.

There is a danger that generalisations might not be interpreted as an indefinite statement containing a range of possibilities. For example,

the confluence of a stream and a river is a most likely place to find a feeding trout, yet at times an insect-rich stream enters a river along a very turbulent reach excluding the possibility of a feeding fish. In contrast, the junction of two waterways sometimes occurs in the eye of a pool in the mainstream. The likelihood of finding trout in such a situation is extremely high.

On the first Sunday of the 1980 fishing season, I fished the Inanga-hua River near Reefton. The light of early morning made spotting difficult, but as the sun rose higher trout began to appear, as suspected, along the edges. About midday when visibility was very good I stumbled upon the situation described above. A clear, gentle stream met the main river in the eye of the pool. To make this an even more desirable lie the stream was like crystal while the river had a tolerable coloration. A careful, lingering stalk revealed not one trout, not two, but a line of five.

The immediate thought was: "Begin with the downstream one and work up to take all five." The closest fish obeyed the rule that early in the season they are easy to hook but it also shattered my wild hope of 100% success by pressing upstream to scare the others despite considerable side tension of straining rod and line. Fortunately I did not suffer the irony of losing "number one" as well, although his mediocre condition ultimately earned him freedom as he was returned to fatten for another day.

Before describing or identifying some of the most likely feeding lies of trout in a river I should explain the terms used. Thus you will be able to recognise the specific areas referred to.

Rapids: In a variety of ways a river flows from rapid to pool and then into another rapid. These vary in their width velocity and turbulence but are invariably the swiftest and most turbulent stretches of a river.

Pools: These, too, show many forms but may be thought of as slower, deeper stretches between the rapids. The place where a rapid runs into a pool and its velocity begins to decrease is called the *head of the pool* while at the opposite end, where the bed is wider and shallower and shelves upwards, it is termed the *tail.* At the head of a pool there is an angular zone between the fast flowing current and the bank. This section of quieter flow is called the *eye of the pool.*

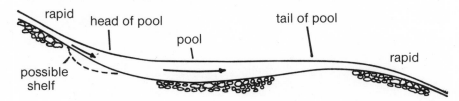

Illust. 12
Profile of a river.

Also at the head of many pools a *steep shelf* can be observed extending across the river bed. At this point the depth increases suddenly. This condition shows frequently where a rapid runs into a high bank and

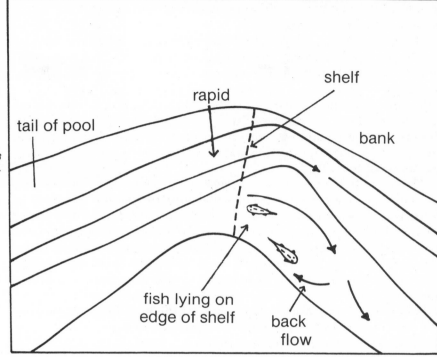

Illust. 13
Shelf formation at a bend.

then the flow turns through about 70°-90° and runs into the pool.

Usually a rapid will run into a pool but this does not always occur. Sometimes beyond a rapid the depth does not increase markedly and a long stretch of water punctuated by rocky obstructions precedes the next rapid. Such a section of river is called a *reach*.

Photo 6
Shelf across riverbed —
note position of fish.

Photo 7
Parts of a river.

Where to Look

The flow of a river can be divided into two kinds, turbulent or laminar. *Turbulent flow* implies swift current which on impact with obstructions tumbles and swirls resulting in movement in several directions. The form of turbulence is determined by the slope and nature of the river bed thus careful observation of the surface movement can disclose much about what lies beneath. *Laminar flow* means movement in one direction only with low velocity. Laminar flow in the literal sense rarely occurs in a river, but as some stretches approach the condition the term is used here in a comparative sense.

Rocks impeding the flow in a reach or along the edge of a pool sometimes stand alone. Sometimes they are grouped or sometimes form a bar. Whichever of these is the case the resulting effect on the current is similar. Directly downstream of the deflector is termed the *lee side*. If two such rocks stand about 10-15 metres apart (in line with the flow) and both affect the current between them, a *pocket* of slower flow is formed.

Current can be similarly diverted by gravel or rock bars extending

Photo 8
Parts of a river.

Photo 10
Turbulent flow.

Photo 9
Laminar flow.

27

Photo 11
Bank extension.

from the bank. Downstream from these *bank extensions* a current congruous to the eye of a pool results.

During four months over two fishing seasons I took notes each time I went fishing. The objective was to note the position of every feeding fish I saw and endeavour to relate each to a specific niche. The results of this survey are summarised in Tables 1, 2 and 3.

Feeding Position	creek mouth	tail of pool	eye of pool	lee side of rock	lee of jutting bank	in front of rock	stomach of pool (surface)
Number observed	78	66	192	114	78	114	54
Percentage of total	10	8	26	20	10	20	7

Table 1   FEEDING TROUT SEEN OCT 1-DEC 1 (Two seasons)

Feeding Position	creek mouth	tail of pool	eye of pool	lee side of rock	lee of jutting bank	in front of rock	stomach of pool
Number observed	42	42	204	138	54	144	156
Percentage of total	5	5	25	16	7	17	19

Table 2   FEEDING TROUT SEEN DEC 1-FEB 1 (Two seasons)

Percentage for entire period	8	7	26	17	8	18	14

Table 3   PERCENTAGES FOR 4 MONTHS (Two seasons)

Care should be taken in reading the tables as they are meant as an approximate guide only. There were several difficulties in compiling the figures which highlight the inaccuracies of the results.

1. The figures relate to 9 rivers in the Nelson district. I enjoy most of my fishing in back country waters such as Buller, Wangapeka, Maruia, Matakitaki, etc., so the results are more specific to such waters.
2. The general water conditions were different for tables 1 and 2. The rivers were clear when all results were taken but spring flows (greater volume) prevailed for Table 1. Predominantly summer low flows existed for the second table.
3. In searching for feeding fish I tend to concentrate my attention in certain parts of a river (i.e., those shown on the tables) and must therefore miss other foragers. This tends to bias the results.
4. Placing things in categories, especially when the categories themselves are extremely varied, can lead to misinterpretation.
5. It is a very small sample (1476 trout).
6. The figures were all taken in the middle of the day (9 a.m.-3 p.m.) and relate to this time only. A different pattern would emerge in the evening.

Despite many drawbacks the tables do provide an intriguing picture.

The outstanding features are:
1. Overall 26% of the feeding fish I saw were in an eye position.
2. A large percentage fed in front of rocks.
3. Similarly large percentages were harboured in the lee of rocks and in the lee of extended banks.
4. There was a noticeable increase in the number of surface feeders in the centre of pools as summer heightened.

Photo 12
Lee of a jutting bank.

1. THE EYE OF THE POOL	Illustrations 13, 15, 16, 17, 20, 21, 22 Photos 7, 8, 14, 48
2. THE TAIL OF THE POOL	Illustrations 12, 23, 24 Photos 7, 8, 50
3. IN FRONT OF A ROCK	Illustrations 25, 28, 29, 30 Photos 17, 18, 19
4. IN THE LEE OF A BANK EXTENSION	Illustrations 31, 32, 33, 34, 35 Photos 11, 12, 38
5. IN THE LEE OF AN OBSTRUCTION	Illustrations 30, 37, 38, 39, 40
6. THE POCKET BETWEEN ROCKS	Illustration 36 Photo 49
7. THE SHELF AT THE HEAD OF THE POOL	Photo 6
8. CONFLUENCE OF A STREAM AND RIVER	Illustration 14 Photo 5

Photo 13
Pocket between rocks.

From this brief outline of river configuration I would like the reader to extract eight niches in particular. At least some of the eight can be isolated in all rivers. Each has proven to be a favoured feeding lie. In some rivers one or other may be preferred but as a general gule they should all be approached carefully.

The Eye Of A Pool

Previously the eye was described as an angular zone of quiet water at the head of a pool. Examples are shown in photographs 7, 8 and 14 while generalisations about the flow are drawn in illustrations 20 and 21.

Photo 14
Eye of the pool.

Illust. 14
Trout lying at stream
mouth.

I have no hesitation in describing the eye as *the prime feeding position*. Fish are sometimes found feeding in the lee of a rock or occasionally in front of a rock or in the tail of a pool but frequently would be a more suitable word to describe the likelihood of finding them in the eye. Furthermore this is consistent for the vast majority of rivers.

The head of each pool has an eye, but the form of that eye varies considerably.

When a river flows from one pool into a rapid then down to another pool in a straight line, then two *eyes* will exist. This condition is well illustrated in photograph 7 and illustration 15 below. More often as a rapid runs into a pool, the river changes the direction of its course. In this case only one eye is found, on the inside of the curve. The nature of the eye bears a relationship to the magnitude of the directional change.

If a river turns through a small angle then the current in the eye, although considerably slower than outstream, is predominantly in the same direction.

30

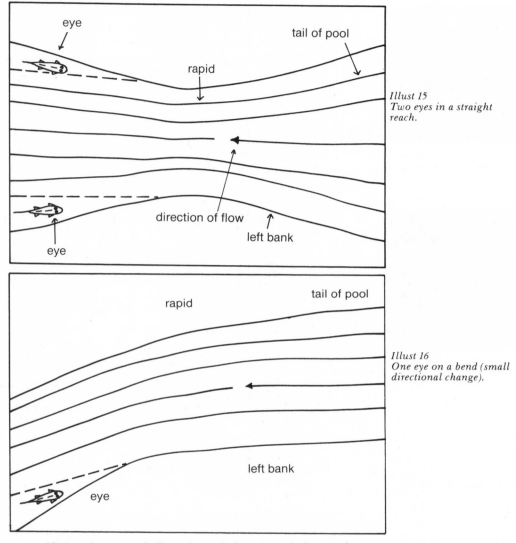

Illust 15
Two eyes in a straight reach.

Illust 16
One eye on a bend (small directional change).

In contrast, if the change of direction of the river is large then a *backcurrent* results. Where this condition exists an angler should approach with extreme caution because a feeding trout will be facing downstream in the direction of approach and probably cruising.

Between these extremes an abundant number of possibilities remain.

In the situation where little or no backcurrent exists the angler should first concentrate his attention along the line of current change. Then, the entire angular zone should be scanned.

If I searched the eye of a pool and could not discern a moving shape or shadow then I would look again. If still none appeared I would move on upstream, not because there were no trout but because more probably I failed to see them.

To aid understanding as to why the eye of a pool (and other niches) holds feeding trout a number of graphic illustrations have been provided.

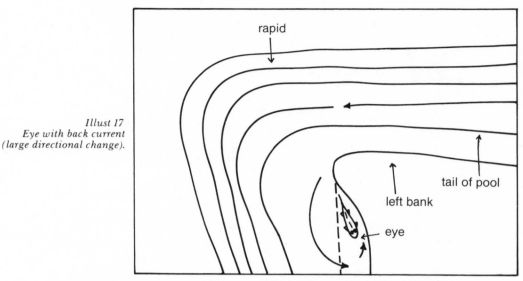

Illust 17
Eye with back current
(large directional change).

Illustration 18 shows what a typical channel would look like if an angler was looking upstream at a cross section of the river. The most outstanding feature in this generalisation is that the *flow is displaced to one side*. This means that the slope of the bed is steeper on one side than the other. The deepest part of the river is therefore closer to one bank.

Illustration 19 shows how the velocity of the current varies across the channel.

On the graph the vertical axis depicts the speed of flow (in metres per

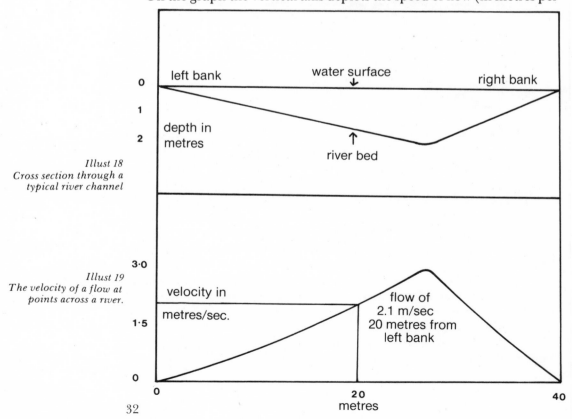

Illust 18
Cross section through a
typical river channel

Illust 19
The velocity of a flow at
points across a river.

second) while on the horizontal axis 0 represents the left bank and 40 shows the distance to the right bank. The graph itself shows that the current of the river increases gradually as one moves from the left bank and the maximum velocity approximately coincides with the point of maximum depth — closer to the right bank.

Illustration 20 is an aerial view of a river as it passes out of the tail of a pool, through a rapid and changes direction into a new pool creating an eye. The dotted line indicates the position where the cross section of illustration 21 was taken.

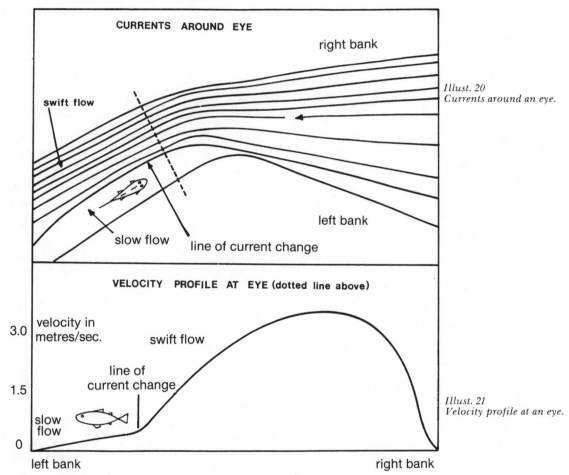

Illust. 20
Currents around an eye.

Illust. 21
Velocity profile at an eye.

On illustration 20 the closeness of the lines suggests the relative velocity of the flow. So, in the tail of the pool (on the right of the graph) the velocity is relatively slow, but then moving leftwards the speed increases and the flow becomes displaced to the right bank.

The graph below illustration 21, represents the relative flows across the river at the section indicated by the dotted line in illustration 20. At the left bank the flow is 0 and it increases slowly away from the left bank (in the eye region). Some distance out from the left bank there is a distinct point at which the velocity changes (increases) rapidly and continues to get faster to reach its maximum close to the right bank.

33

Relatively close to the right bank the flow is still quite swift.

For the stalking angler the important feature is the relative flow between the eye and the remainder of the river. In the eye the flow *is slow* and nearly laminar. Beyond the eye the velocity increases very quickly. Between the mainflow and eye a distinct line is formed. As mentioned earlier, it is along this line (but on the inner edge) that trout can be expected to lie. They choose to feed in this location for three main reasons: (a) they are lying in a sluggish current and are therefore not expending much energy; (b) drifting food tends to accumulate along this line; (c) they are within easy reach of the safety of deeper, faster water if danger should approach.

Photo 15
Lines of current change.

Photo 16
Lines of current change.

Illust. 22
Trout lying in eye of a
pool.

The Tail of a Pool

If our centre of interest was fishing to the evening rise or if we were discussing fishing a river in a fresh, then more time would be devoted to the tail of a pool. In these circumstances, trout for various reasons drift back down the pool to feed. But as daytime anglers we cannot expect the same numbers to feed in this niche.

There is no doubt in the minds of all fishermen that the far bank is infinitely more promising than the occupied one. Hence river crossings are frequent. The easiest place to cross the river to the new attraction is the tail. As illustrations 23 and 24 and photographs 7 and 8 show, the relative depth at this point is less than elsewhere in the pool while the current velocity is also low, even in the centre. The physical reason for these conditions is that the bed is wider, allowing the flow is spread further.

On illustration 23 the horizontal line represents the water's surface, while the curved line below is the river bed stretching from left bank to right. The accompanying graph (illustration 24) demonstrates the speed of flow at all points across this part of a river. The speed of flow (shown by the curved line) increases slowly as one moves from left bank to right but importantly never reaches a high peak. The maximum velocity is normally slightly closer to one bank (in this case the right) and coincides with the point of greatest depth.

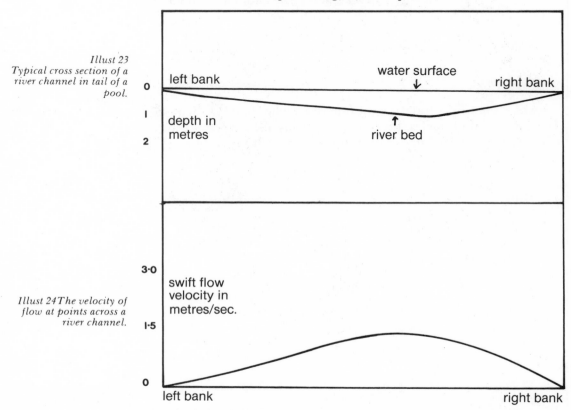

Illust 23 Typical cross section of a river channel in tail of a pool.

Illust 24 The velocity of flow at points across a river channel.

A principle which I hope will emerge as being of utmost importance in determing where trout may be is their attraction to *lines of distinct current change* where the flow is fast on one side of the line and slow on the other.

I mention this here because the tail is one niche where the principle is *not* of major importance. Because no specific line exists it is more difficult to direct your attention to any particular position across the tail.

The velocity is slowest at the edges (see illustration 24) so perhaps the search should be there first. The edges would also be closest to your approach giving these feeding fish a greater chance of detecting your presence.

Although the majority of feeding trout in the tail of a pool are observed near the banks, it is not uncommon for them to be in mid-stream.

As the flow across the tail of a pool is of a less disturbed nature trout are spotted with relative ease. But remember, *if you can see a trout easily then the converse is almost certainly true.* It is probably this unobstructed vision that the fish have that encourages them to venture so far from the security of the pool.

Remember, too, that if you scare one fish it is very likely it will make its escape at high speed alarming anything in its path. With visibility so clear such a path is wide in the tail of a pool. Tables 1, 2 and 3 show a comparatively small percentage of feeding fish in the tail of a pool. This low figure is partially accounted for by the perilous nature of the niche, although inaccuracy may also have played a part.

In Front Of A Rock (or other obstruction)

I was taught by a fraternity of fishermen who directed their efforts downstream of obstacles, thus for most of my fishing years I did the same. But as my stalking skills improved and self-teaching predominated I observed many fish feeding upstream of rocks.

Illust. 25
Trout positioned in front of rock.

Last season Dave Lyttle and I returned regularly to a short reach of the Upper Buller. Apart from the ever present trout the main attraction was the broken nature of the flow which ran enthusiastically around numerous sizeable boulders. Our search for feeding fish was normally a survey of the edges out of the typical Buller torrent.

On one occasion Dave was floating his fly downstream when it was caught in a fast current and carried out towards a large boulder which dammed up a noticeable wave on its upstream side. As Dave was about to commence his backcast and retrieve the sinking molefly a large snout broke the surface in pursuit. The reflex of the rising wrist was too far advanced. The dripping fly jerked from the trout's hungry mouth. Usually in this situation the trout would drift from view leaving a frustrated angler gazing at the once occupied feeding lie. The fly would be either hooked in a bush high above the despondent fisherman or floating aimlessly and unheeded downstream.

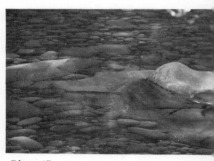

Photo 17
In front of a rock.

This time the shape remained and was now so obvious it seemed remarkable that we had missed seeing it before. In fairness to our

Angler hooked in bushes behind.

ability, the reason we had left the fish undisturbed was that a cursory glance had ruled the flow too fast to be considered a holding place. Obviously our judgement was wrong.

Dave retrieved his fly from an offending shrub and sought the best possible footing in the surging flow. When a new fly pattern neared the same fish it was accepted without hesitation. With the elements on the fish's side the result of the furious battle was a fisherman's cliché, 'he got away'.

We returned a week later and a third offering was taken equally hungrily as was a fourth later still. On each occasion the fish used the current to carry its estimated three kilogram frame downstream to freedom.

It would not surprise me if the same fish, considerably larger and wiser now, does not dwell in the same reach today.

Other writers have also noted the importance of the upstream side of a rock as a holding position.

In his book "The Complete Book of Fly Fishing", Larry Solomon wrote, 'Most people think that the best lie for a trout is behind a rock. This may seem logical, but I have seen more good fish holding in front of rocks than behind.'

This opinion is substantiated by an opinion of Clark and Goddard who wrote '. . . it is perfectly true that trout often lie in wait for food on

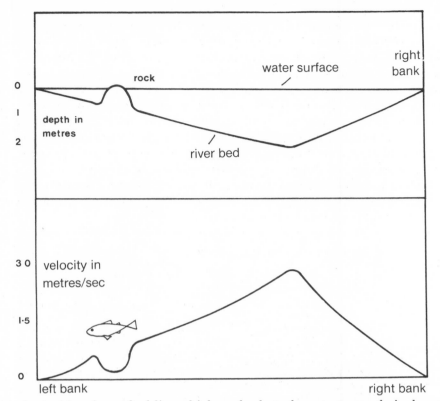

Illust 28
Typical channel cross
section with rock in bed.

Illust 29
The effect of a rock on the
velocity of flow.

the inside edges of eddies which such obstacles create, on their down-stream sides. But far more often — except in very fast water — the trout lie in front of rocks, and to the sides of them. And the man who has concentrated his attention behind such things has been missing at least half of the fish on offer.'

Having emphasised the importance of the upstream side of an ob-struction as a feeding lie I would like to stress one other point before outlining the reasons trout seek this position. To the experienced angler it is obvious that only a small number of obstructions are suitable for the trout's needs. The inexperienced need to be taught this lesson.

When considering which boulders are most likely to harbour a trout ahead, the needs of a fish should be recounted: (a) an abundant food supply; (b) proximity to the safety of deep water and cover; (c) shelter from fast energy-sapping flow.

All obstructions to flow satisfy the third need to a greater or lesser extent but the ones which should receive the stalking angler's attention are those which fulfil the first two needs as well. Assuming that there is a constant supply of insects, and safety is nearby, illustrations 29 and 30 demonstrate the hydrological suitability of the lie.

Illustration 30 is a view of the obstruction from above. Where the lines are closest together the current is quickest. The wide spacing *ahead of the obstruction* emphasises a cushioning of the current in which the velocity is considerably *lower* than nearby on all sides.

Illustrations 28 and 29 show the same idea in profile view. Illustra-tion 28 is a cross section of the river with a rock in the bed. The effect

Photo 18
Casting to a trout
in front of a rock.

Photo 19
Current in front of a rock.

which the rock has on the flow is pictured in illustration 29. *A distinct decline in velocity appears in front of the rock* and punctuates an otherwise increasing flow as the centre of the river is approached. Photographs present one example of the lie being described. In this case the rock does not fringe a pool but edges a straight reach.

Sometimes such an obstruction would be further out in the current; more frequently its position would be closer to the shore. The possibilities are numerous. Many would be rocks with no water flowing over the top, while others would lie submerged. Assuming a refuge is near for disturbed trout, all should be approached most cautiously.

Tables 1, 2 and 3 suggest that one fifth of feeding trout lie upstream from obstacles. This large percentage speaks for itself. It is a prime lie, and stalking fishermen treat it as such.

Illust 30
Relative flow around an obstacle

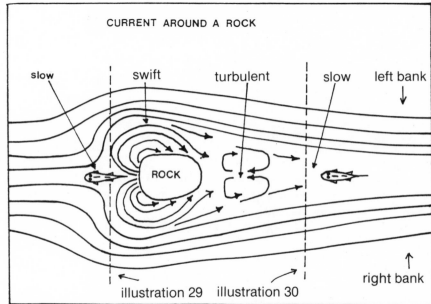

In The Lee Of A Bank Extension

Photo 20
Bank extension.

Bank extensions differ enormously and their effect on the current displays comparative variation. Yet, despite this divergence, one point of similarity exists. A line separating swift and slow flow shows unmistakeably downstream of the protrusion. Thus an environment in which a trout can shelter from energy-sapping flow, while still receiving an abundant food supply, is created.

Bank extensions are often impermeable to the flow (i.e. of a solid nature) forcing the entire current out. The resulting extremes are either turbulence and backflow downsteam, or a small pool of little or no flow.

A more ideal condition is when the extension allows some of the flow to pass through (for example, a bouldery bar). In this case there is less likely to be turbulence downstream yet the water velocity will have been decreased considerably.

40

Trout lying in lee of bank extension.

The effect which obstructions have on flow is repeatedly revealed by the nature of the river bed downstream of the obstruction. The distinctly slower current allows much finer debris to be dropped. Therefore the line of current change along which the trout lie can be observed by ascertaining the line separating coarse and fine bedload.

The Lee Of An Obstruction

Using a fly, and dry fly in particular, would be my first choice every time in seeking to catch a trout. But my love of deceiving these marvellous creatures is such that if conditions necessitate a change to some other form of deceit then I have no hesitation in altering my strategy.

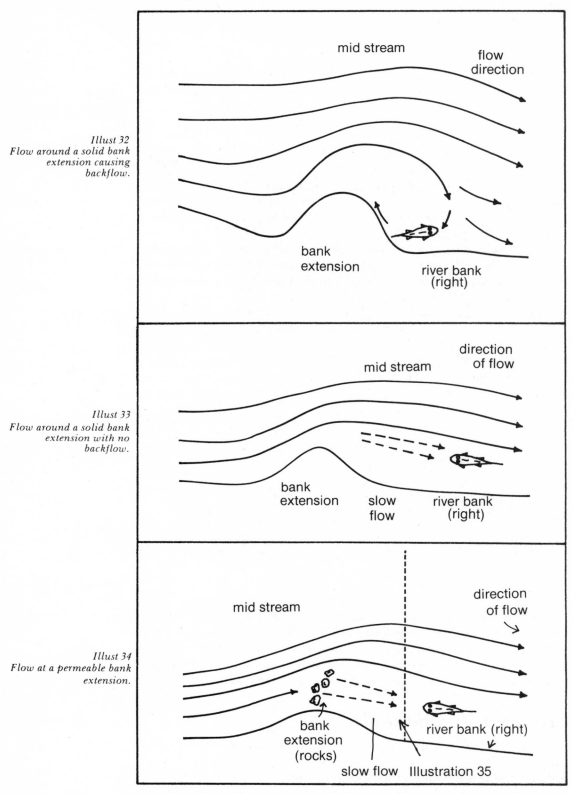

Illust 32
Flow around a solid bank extension causing backflow.

mid stream

flow direction

bank extension

river bank (right)

Illust 33
Flow around a solid bank extension with no backflow.

mid stream

direction of flow

bank extension

slow flow

river bank (right)

Illust 34
Flow at a permeable bank extension.

mid stream

direction of flow

bank extension (rocks)

slow flow

Illustration 35

river bank (right)

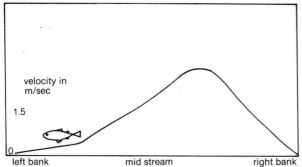

Illust 35
The effect of a bank extension on a velocity of flow.

A fresh in a river with discoloured water invariably dictates employment of methods other than the dry fly. Some know the effectiveness of a floating worm at this time although I prefer to assemble my threadline outfit.

In early December, several years ago, I drove to the middle reaches of the Motueka River and found it swollen and partially discoloured. The conditions were ideal for threadlining. There was no time wasted in preparation. I was at the water's edge smartly and the first cast was made with total anticipation.

Flooded rivers carry their volume at high velocity so pockets of quieter water are in strong contrast and therefore reveal themselves plainly. The first reclusive lie I came to showed downstream from a large rock. The water into which I directed my lure to swing was *not directly downstream of the rock, where inhospitable turbulence appeared on the*

A trout lying downstream of log.

43

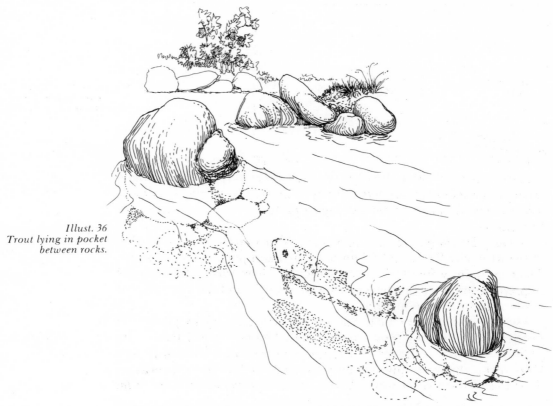

Illust. 36
Trout lying in pocket
between rocks.

surface, but about eight or ten metres adrift of it. Despite high expectation the strike of an eager trout was still electrifying. That moment with a threadline is akin to the take with a fly or nymph and is the moment of greatest satisfaction — the triumph! What follows is a bonus. On this occasion I was treated to an unparalleled display of aeronautics and water-walking as the trout fought impressively to regain its freedom. This time I was the victor.

Eight trout were landed that day and many more lost. Of the eight, seven were hooked on the lee side of a rock, which is testimony to the importance of this position as a feeding lie even in extreme river conditions.

Expose a person to a relentless, icy wind and the reaction would normally be in two stages. First the back would be turned and then shelter sought behind the nearest windbreak. Instinct and experience tell us the relief that awaits there. Similarly, leaves and other wind-blown debris will come to rest downwind of any obstacle while even very fine bedload will halt downstream of a current obstruction. Trout also instinctively know the nullifying effects of obstructions to river flow and actively seek the resulting refuge.

The general effect which a barrier has on the current is to slow the flow velocity for a short distance upstream and *a much longer distance downstream*. The extent of the downstream zone varies considerably with differences in obstacle size and shape, water depth and velocity and whether the obstacle is fully or partially immersed. As it would be an impossible task to describe all these variations, I will demonstrate the extremes only.

1. A large boulder partially submerged in fast deep flow.

Fish in this case would be expected *a distance downstream beyond the most turbulent section of flow.* Both surface and bottom feeders seek this situation.

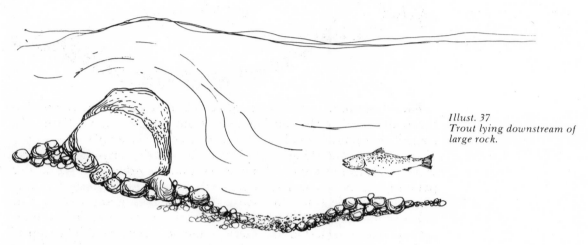

*Illust. 37
Trout lying downstream of large rock.*

2. A smaller rock or shelf on the river bed.

Here a fish would sit very close to the obstruction and right on the river bed.

3. A bouldery bed.

Fish would sit on or close to the river bed and close behind a rock. Slight turbulence would occur all along the bed.

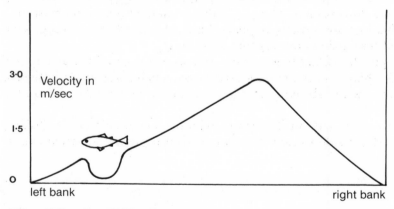

*Illust 38
The effect of a rock on the downsteam flow.*

The Moving Window

The passage of water as it spills into a pool is soon slowed by a deepening and widening bed. But as it slows it still rolls along at the surface — the rolling reflecting the bouldery nature of the bed below. Even in bright sunlight such turbulent waters are difficult to search. Yet search we must because the zone midstream in a pool where the flow is being checked often harbours feeding trout.

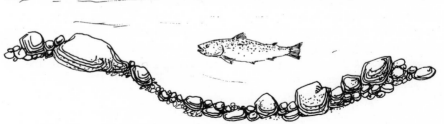

Trout lying in depression.

Knowing this has proven advantageous on numerous occasions. Recently my brother Ho and I enjoyed a day on the Travers River. We stalked on opposite banks to cover as much river as possible. In one place I scrambled along a steep bush-covered face high above a pool while Ho lingered a short distance back on the other side. He waited patiently for me to check the pool because being high above the water and in the shade I had the better chance of seeing any feeding fish.

It was one of those places where the initial glance revealed nothing, yet experience suggested that there should be a trout there. The rippled and rolling surface of the pool proved difficult to see through but occasionally a flat moving window would appear at the surface and provide visibility right to the river bed. Concentrating upstream, my eyes caught an anticipated window. I followed it down with my eyes, rejoicing because its shape widened as it moved.

Deep down on a bouldery bed a large trout was revealed — its image astonishingly clear — but then it disappeared again as the window dissipated downstream. The next window verified the trout's position. From his location on the opposite bank Ho could see nothing, so I watched his casting and directed accordingly.

Two people fishing together like this is exciting and rewarding for both. On this occasion I had the advantage of being able to see both fish and angler while Ho enjoyed the anticipation of the take and battle ahead.

Finally, even without the aid of a window, I could discern the fish as it glided from side to side. Ho's large nymph pitched upstream time

Trout lying on bouldery bed.

after time but it passed over the trout seemingly unnoticed. Ho concluded that, in the deep fast water, the nymph was not sinking close enough to be attractive, so he resolved to add a little more nylon to his tippet which would allow a cast to be made further upstream.

With renewed hope the battle continued, the fisherman hopeful, the fish unaware. Casting was obviously more difficult because the power arc of the rod increased and an occasional backcast broke the water behind. Diminishing finesse and precision are acceptable when success results. Thus we were rewarded. The nymph plopped well upstream and slightly to one side. The fish rose higher than it had for naturals — a common sign of an interested trout.

The line stopped abruptly. Ho tightened, and revelled at the struggling weight at the other end. The power of the fish was astonishing as it bored upstream then continued through the white water towards the next pool. Refuge behind a huge boulder halted the fish's progress and allowed Ho to retrieve most of his line and approach the fish. Another lunge and the fish retreated downstream back into the pool, where it made for the far bank which it hugged as it dragged the line in a wide arc downstream. Again line was retrieved and closer contact made with the trout. Yet nothing could be done to edge it to the shore. The reason for Ho's lack of control was soon apparent. In the clarity of the lower reaches of the pool we could see that the nymph was not in the fish's mouth but hooked into the dorsal fin.

How a hook can become imbedded in a fin or tail is a mystery, but I have witnessed it several times. Invariably the ensuing battle is long with the fish possessing unusual power and total control.

Ho's fish was immovable. It sulked along the depths for some time before initiating its freedom. Apparently indifferent to proceedings where we were, the fish made an unchecked run down towards the next pool. The nymph tore free. Justice was served.

Without the aid of the moving window we would not have seen that fish, or several others, that day. On days of poor light these corridors of visibility can be the only means of spotting trout on some reaches. They are common but require patience and slow progress to be used profitably.

Another Consideration

From the river bed to the water surface the velocity is not uniform. If measurements were taken of this depth-velocity relationship in different places in a river, then variation would show. Yet despite some contrast a pattern does emerge. The pattern is a parabolic curve with *the maximum speed somewhere in the top third of a channel.*

Of importance for the trout fisherman is the *slower zone near the river bed* and perhaps to a much lesser extent a *slight decrease at the surface.*

The river bed and the surface are *places of food concentration* which alone makes them attractive to trout but lower water speed in these zones may help to explain an absence of feeding fish in between.

An exciting sight for a fly fisherman is to see a trout leave the security of the depths of a pool and undertake the long journey to the surface to intercept a tiny fly. It is even more thrilling if that fly is tied to a thin length of nylon!

Illust 41
The relative velocity of
flow at points from suface
to bed.

One brilliantly fine summer's day I lunched with friends on the banks of a crystal clear Karamea River. We sat beside a pool which we estimated to be more than 3 metres deep. In addition to the singing of bellbirds and the curiosity of robins we were entertained by a trout which fed continuously. The remarkable feature of its behaviour was that it rested on the river bed and each tiny morsel of food it chose floated on the surface. Each ascent seemed an endless affair but not once was there a rejection. The trout's mind seemed made up the moment it left the bottom.

It wasn't long before one of our party suggested I should tempt our friend with a molefly. No further prompting was needed.

Deep pools often mean steep banks and difficult casting. It is a price one often has to pay to afford a friendly audience a grandstand view. This occasion was no exception.

Positioning myself on a narrow ledge at water level I checked behind to see what could provide further hindrance to my backcast. The way was clear. From this less elevated stand the fish was barely discernible but as it rose to another lightly bobbing fly it took shape clearly. I waited until the resting lie was reoccupied then set my 2.2 metre rod into action. As delicately as possible I placed the fly on the water a few feet upstream from the taking position. Again the shape eased from the river bed and rose effortlessly toward the surface. There was no doubt about the events that were to follow — no doubt, that was, providing I could contain my excitement and refrain from tightening too soon. I will not mention the number of times I have made this mistake, but instead boast of success this time. Not only were we treated to a marvellous view of the feeding fish and the take but also the calm, clear waters allowed us to observe the jinking and diving of the fish as it battled for its life.

The trout's very fine condition demonstrated that it rarely wasted energy in obtaining its food. The long journey it undertook from bed to surface may suggest otherwise, but consider for a moment the relative velocity on the river bed (especially in deep pools) compared to higher, and the trout's choice makes sense especially with the security of depth as a bonus.

3

What To Look For

Observing other sports, as a complete novice, has aided my understanding of the problems encountered by relative newcomers to fishing.

One friend is an enthusiastic pigeon fancier. His dedication, or more correctly, fanaticism, encouraged me to join him and patiently wait and search for returning racers. I did this on numerous occasions, always scanning the skies in the hope that I would be first to spot the leading bird. Yet, despite many efforts, the birds were always either pointed out to me, or about to land on the loft before I saw them. I lacked a trained eye and the necessary instinct.

The flight of a pigeon is subtly different from that of other birds. Its purpose and speed distinguish it from the floating gulls, hovering larks or hedge-hopping blackbirds. The fancier can spot this instantly and is not distracted by unfamiliar movements.

Novice fishermen or anglers who have not relied on spotting when gaining their past successes are plagued by similar inabilities when trying to discern trout in a stream. Only hours of practice will gradually instill the skills and eliminate distractions, thus directing attention to feeding fish.

In this context I am not talking about the obvious trout which warily cruise flat back waters and calm lake edges, or those which drift over sand beds of clear calm pools. These fish are easy for all to see. The trout the stalking angler seeks inhabit, by instinct, niches rendering them more difficult to see.

In fact, what is sought is not the image of a complete fish. Look for this and failure is likely. Instead the eyes must probe and hunt for a number of subtleties. An outline of these subtleties follows but remember that although they have been listed here it is invariably a blend of several which expose a fish.

Photo 22
An obvious cruiser.

Factors Suggesting The Presence Of A Trout

1. Line
2. Shape
3. Colour
4. Shadow
5. Fins, tail and mouth
6. Movement
7. River bed disturbance
8. Sound
9. Dimple

Line

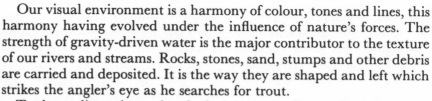

Photo 23
An obvious cruiser.

Our visual environment is a harmony of colour, tones and lines, this harmony having evolved under the influence of nature's forces. The strength of gravity-driven water is the major contributor to the texture of our rivers and streams. Rocks, stones, sand, stumps and other debris are carried and deposited. It is the way they are shaped and left which strikes the angler's eye as he searches for trout.

To the undiscerning a river bed may appear disorganised. But close scrutiny reveals sand, and fine grains often predominate on inner curves and coarser material resists flow in the faster currents at the outer sides. Freestone beds tend to be flattened as this repose offers least resistance to the energy of flow.

There is also a uniformity in the size of material on a river bed. For example, in high country reaches of a river there exists a greater proportion of large stones and rocks, while downstream stretches harbour more fine material.

Photo 24
*Larger rocks and stones
characteristic of the upper
reaches of a river.*

It would be impossible to describe even a small percentage of the patterns one could find but these above are mentioned to demonstrate how they can be used to assist in discerning the line of a trout.

River bed material is laid down so that it offers least resistance to the current but rarely do the rocks, etc., match the trout's ability to lie directly in line with the current. Unless a fish is moving it will never alter this angle. In addition to this consistency the line which an angler is searching for is of reasonably uniform size. In South Island waters most fish are in the 38cm-55cm range.

Feeding trout rarely remain in direct contact with the river bed. As the bed tends to be naturally flattened the line of a feeding fish is therefore rendered slightly more apparent.

Shape

Because most stalking is done by moving upstream the majority of trout are viewed from a similar angle — from behind. In addition, as mentioned above, trout consistently lie exactly in line with the current. These regularities mean we are presented with a relatively uniform shape which often contrasts with the shapes of its surrounds. On a river bed there is infinite variation in the shape of individual rocks. Trout, however, are always elongated and torpedo shaped.

I know one Southland angler who will never forget a trout he recognised by its shape. His province has a reputation for cool, showery weather. Although this is a reasonably accurate and consistent summary, there are days, particularly inland, when the heat is almost unbearable. On such a day the angler used his boat to explore inaccessible places on Lake Mavora. Weed banks, stream mouths, secluded bays and other areas of promise were reached by boat then patrolled on foot. All revealed nothing. A blazing sun and windless atmosphere coupled with apparently lifeless waters reduced the angler's enthusiasm quickly. With increasing discomfort his thoughts drifted from fishing to swimming.

He looked across the lake to distant campers. They were barely visible so he removed all of his clothes and placed them with his fishing gear on the gravel. His bureaucratic feet led him daintily past the boat towards the water's edge. He was tentatively about to test the tem-

Photo 25 & 26
Fine material
characteristic of a lowland
river.

51

*Photo 27
Typical torpedo shape of a
trout.*

perature with a toe when a distant, familiar shape caught his eye. It was still 10 metres away, foraging along the shallows but edging closer. Unbelievable! A morning's fishing with rod in hand had been futile. Now, with rod 5 metres away, a chance presented itself. But it was not possible to retreat without being seen. The only immediate course of action was to lie as low and still as possible and wait for the fish to pass, then pursue later.

Few people sunbathe near our beech forests. It is not the lack of sunshine but the relentless, infuriating sandflies. Their instincts never fail as our fisherman promptly discovered. There he crouched, naked and vulnerable. Moving, or swatting insects, was inconceivable. The trout lingered, then shifted closer, nosing the lake bed and breaking the surface with its tail. Its passing seemed to take an eternity, but it remained undisturbed because it still fed as it stole away.

The fisherman tiptoed to his clothes and hastily covered himself. By the time he was equipped for action the trout had disappeared. Reckoning it would repeat the beat the fisherman sat scanning the water expectantly. Five minutes passed. Then ten. Not a movement, not a shape. Twenty minutes was the limit. The angler pushed his boat back into the water and dejectedly departed. No fish, no swim and itching in many places!

Colour

In their fight for survival wild animals have evolved numerous ways of camouflaging themselves. Matching the colours of the environment is common and a method successfully adopted by trout.

Trout have the ability to develop tones matching those of the immediate vicinity — which means that within a trout family wide colour variation may exist. For example, a brown trout living in a brackish bush stream is often dark alongs its back and distinctly brown on its flanks, while a brown trout in clearer waters may exhibit lighter tones. A trout taken from one environment and put into a new one will soon change colour to blend.

Looking for colour, then, would seem a poor aid in spotting trout, yet surprisingly there are times when it is colour which strikes the eye first in identifying a fish. The distinctive green-backed browns of the Wangapeka immediately spring to mind — although maybe they don't care about being seen because they are so difficult to catch.

Another subtlety about colour is that a river bed is an accumulation of varying tones of rock and algae. A trout cannot match all of these at one time, so as it moves gently from side to side it continually exposes a minor variance.

Shadow And The Disappearing Bed

Colour may be the initial factor disclosing the presence of some trout while others harmonize with their environment so well that they are nearly impossible to see. Yet despite the enormous advantage these fish possess they can still be recognised — not so much as an image, rather because of the effect their presence has on the river bed.

The first effect is that as a fish sways from side side selecting drifting nymphs it simultaneously hides and reveals the stones below it. Thus it appears as a moving ghost.

On a bright sunny day a further benefit appears for the angler. Trout wavering in the current commonly feed off the bed, hence they cast a shadow. A trained eye can sometimes be alerted by this alone.

*Photo 28
Darker tail and dorsal fin.*

Fins, Tail And Mouth

Though nature continually astonishes us with perfections in pattern and function, equally surprising are occasional inexplicable blemishes. As mentioned, trout have evolved a delicate coloration offering concealment. Most retain uniformity in colour (dorsally) from head to tail, but others have obviously darker fins and tails, which can offer an angler sufficient evidence to arouse a *more careful* look.

Other acute hints to a trout's presence are a momentary flash of white from the underside of a turning body, and, occasionally, even the opening of a mouth will display a glimpse of white.

Movement

When the presence of a trout is suspected in a river it may be clues offered by line, colour, shape, etc; but the feature which ultimately leads us to the conclusion that it is a trout is *movement*. Sometimes the whole shape will move, sometimes it will be just the movement of fins and tail. At other times it will be a moving shadow or disappearing image.

River Bed Disturbance

Where river gravel is fine and the bed relatively stable the stones in summer change their colour to shades of green and brown. This coloration is due to the growth of algae. Trout, as they hover above the gravel, wave their tails from side to side or contact the bed with their bellies. As a result, some stones are displaced, leaving a scar. Being territorial by nature a trout will return to the same place frequently (even when there is no apparent advantage) thus maintaining or increasing the scar.

Because this phenomenon only occurs where there are extensive areas of fine stable gravel it is not often observed. I have noticed this effect most often on the Upper Mataura.

Sound

When a trout takes a surface insect there is usually an associated sound. Ernest Schwiebert observed, "The common suction rise is typical of a good fish in relatively quiet water... there is usually an audible sucking sound, leaving one or two bubbles riding the film. The true suction rise occurs to an insect riding on the current, and the bubbles confirm its surface feeding."

Dimple

On a flat-surfaced pool the disturbance caused by a rising trout is obvious. The initial surface distortion and subsequent widening concentric circles of water drifting downstream remain in view for a relatively long period. In the evening these are expected and often noticed because they are awaited. A stalking angler should be aware of those obvious cases, but equally ready to recognise the same feature at any time of the day and in many types of water. In faster flow the evidence remains only briefly, the circles are more restricted and are soon distorted and engulfed. Recognition therefore requires more acute attention.

4

How To Stalk

With my rod trailing I approached the glassy backwater with caution. Willow trees lined the opposite bank. Visibility was good. Another step, then the movement caught my eye. Approaching me, tail cleaving the surface, was a fine brown. It was so close I could do nothing but freeze — aware that my presence was conspicuous on the open bank. Closer and closer the trout moved, nosing the muddy bed, then I was seen. The fished turned towards the sanctuary of deeper water, increased its speed, then accelerated more to disappear, leaving only a small cloud of muddy water.

"There may be another" I thought, "I'll be better prepared if there is."A short distance away a clump of reeds flourished in the mud — ideal cover to sit behind. Determined to do everything right, I crouched as low as possible behind the cover. My rod, ready for casting, lay nearby flat on the ground. In backwaters trout move long distances so there was no need for me to add to my chances of being seen by moving and seeking fish.

The wait was short. First, a dimple and suck caught my attention, 10 metres away, close to the edge. In the crouch my legs ached, yet I dared not ease the cramp. One movement with the fish so close would be fatal. Assured, unhurried, the trout eased past and gradually added to the distance between us. A cast became possible but in the stillness even the luckiest cast would be unnatural. Instead I waited. With the fish out of sight I flicked a small fly which landed then remained stationary, close to the path taken by the fish. The floating line lay on the mud. Another wait, this time longer, but at last, still unhurried, the fish returned. It was very close before it saw my fly in the shallow water. The take was a most delicate affair unlike the strike that followed. Mud sprayed up from the floating line as it tightened and I was on my feet the instant I felt contact. This success relied on the trout being oblivious to my presence.

See Before Being Seen

The whole purpose of stalking trout is to locate them as they feed, but it is imperative that in doing so the angler remains undetected himself. Trout are wild creatures with a strong sense of self-preservation. If a fisherman alerts this sense then the trout will cease feeding and, most often, quickly disappear.

Superficially the act of stalking and remaining concealed appears a simple matter of stealth and care. In fact, it is a highly complex business.

Some of the intricacies can be outlined and taught by practice, but only hours on the river bank (not an onerous task) will instill them as instincts. Only then is some success assured.

Stalking trout can be likened to a battle in which the trout is a very wary and unpredictable foe. Obviously some preparation on the angler's part in understanding the enemy's defences, strengths and weaknesses, will enhance the chances of victory.

The purpose of chapters one and two was to build a body of information disclosing some hideouts in which trout can be expected to be found and to demonstrate the senses used to maintain safety in the place of refuge. Concentration of attention and searching in the correct places in a river is obviously a positive step towards victory, as is using the weaknesses in the trout's defence.

A trout's defence system (as appropriate to a stalking angler).
1. Camouflage.
2. Excellent eyesight — in front, to the side and above. Particularly sensitive to movement.
3. Colour vision.
4. Excellent hearing.
5. Unpredictable movements. E.g., a trout will sit in one place and feed for a long time then, without warning or apparent motive, turn and swim downstream
6. Feeding positions usually within easy reach of deep or fast water.
7. Timid nature. Give a trout even the slightest indication of danger and defensive behaviour is induced.

Weaknesses in the trout's defence (as appropriate to a stalking angler).
1. The eyes are placed laterally and allow vision in front, to the sides and above, but a blind zone exists behind (low down in particular).
2. Vision outside the water is restricted to some extent, particularly when a fish feeds near to the surface.
3. Trout seek to feed in special places in a river, making them easier to find.
4. Some behaviour is predictable — e.g. territorial behaviour. One trout will feed in the same place day after day; if it is scared off once then more care could be used in the same location later.
5. Within a trout's territory the fish may swim along a regular path. Hence ambush tactics are feasible.
6. Vision from sunlit water into shade is poor, i.e., images in the shade are indistinct.
7. Vision into the sun is difficult.
8. There exists a linear relationship between a trout's sensitivity and an angler's speed of movement, i.e., the slower an angler moves the greater the difficulty a trout has in detecting him.

9. A trout's ability to distinguish between similar tones of colour is considerably less than its ability to discern contrasting tones.

Being aware of these strengths and weaknesses is the key to the angler's attack. If a trout can't see behind, then attack from behind. If a trout sees well up high then stay low. If a trout detects fast movement then move slowly. If a trout can distinguish colour then use camouflage.

It is all so logical yet so difficult to achieve in practice. Difficult because we move too quickly despite knowing we shouldn't. Difficult because we too often give that half chance which is all the trout needs.

What To Wear

A fisherman's clothing should fulfil three purposes it should: 1) assist in locating trout; 2) provide camouflage for the angler; 3) assist in stealth on the river bank.

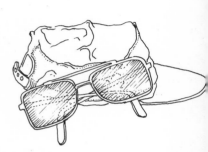

Polaroid glasses and a peaked cap are invaluable aids in improving vision. The importance of polaroids to a stalking angler cannot be overstated, because without their capacity to reduce reflected light from the water surface, visibility into the water would be considerably less.

The effectiveness of polaroids can be enhanced by rotating the lenses after a stretch of river has been scanned. By rotating the lenses another area of reflection will be reduced. Hence sight into depths previously hidden is possible.

When an angler raises and lowers his head position new vistas may similarly emerge.

One has to leave the ever-faithful cap at home just once to realise its importance. Without a lens shader the polaroids are far less effective. If no hat is worn then its function must be performed by the use of arm and hand. Not only is this a tiring pursuit but also the extended elbow and movement of hand and arm offer those half chances of detection on which the trout's survival relies.

The second function of the stalking angler's clothing is to help him blend with the river bank surroundings. In selecting his apparel consideration must be given to the trout's visual ability and to the environment in which the angler is stalking.

As trout are aware of colour then it would be suicidal to wear anything but tones resembling earth, bush or sky. Bright yellows, oranges and reds are beyond consideration. Monotones would rarely be acceptable. If fishing is done along vegetated banks then mottled greens and browns would provide the greatest advantage while light tones of grey and blue would be more suitable when moving on open stony beaches with a low horizon as a background.

Footwear is our third consideration. Whatever provides a fisherman with the quietest passage along the bank or over the river bed is the most ideal, but unfortunately the need for comfort does not always allow this.

Illust. 43
A well dressed fisherman.

Light gym shoes or sneakers are excellent stalking footwear as they provide ultimate stealth; but they have the disadvantage of being less protective to the feet than boots. Also light footwear usually gives less grip than boots on slimy rock beds. Thigh waders are comparatively clumsy, uncomfortable and dangerous, but necessary in icy October or April waters.

Camouflage clothing and suitable footwear are only minor aids to the fisherman. Far more important is the way he conducts his search. A thoughtfully attired stalker, however, has an edge which may help him cross the line between success and failure.

The lies, half-truths and exaggerations at the end of a day's fishing make the time on the river complete. They are told first when meeting a companion at the car and then again, with greater elaboration in the comfort of a home and with some fortification by food and wine.

Invariably these stories tell of one which was fooled by the angler's fly but had the good fortune and luck to escape. Rarely is the 'one that got away' a trout which saw the angler approaching and fled from his blundering foe. Such tales have little appeal to the listener and add nothing to the angler's esteem, yet I'm sure that more get away in this fashion (usually unnoticed) than in any other.

The Upper Mataura is a marvellous place for stalking trout. Many miles of river are available to accommodate hosts of anglers. But be prepared for the Northwesterly wind, which often blows strong and cool. I took a companion to fish at Garston one day and as we neared the river it was obvious we'd have to be well clothed.

As we prepared our gear I discovered I had foolishly left my coat at home. The problem was soon solved as my friend had a spare — a bright yellow "Ministry of Works" style.

Conditions were not ideal for spotting trout so we used a little local knowledge and sought some high banks which allowed us to look down into the water at a more favourable angle. I took the lead as the spotter and within a short time sighted a fat brown feeding in the edge, totally oblivious to the inclement weather. But within moments it was darting for deeper waters. I cursed my luck and moved on. Twenty metres upstream another shape hovered just beneath the surface and moved freely to floating flies. Again, contact was brief. Again, I cursed my luck. After a third had got away in the same fashion I reluctantly admitted that luck had little to do with our lack of success — it was my thoughtless approach with unsuitable clothing.

It was too cold and wet to discard the offending coat completely so I resolved to halve our fishing time by sheltering during the blustery showers then brave brighter moments displaying only a woollen jersey. When I spotted the next fish I half expected to see it flee immediately too but its continued feeding was testimony to my more suitable clothing.

How To Walk

As a general rule, movement when stalking should be 'slow, slower, slowest'. This is necessary for two principal reasons:
1. A stationary person or one moving very slowly has far greater powers of observation than someone moving quickly. Trout are observed by a number of subtleties such as a colour change, a shape, a line, a shadow or a movement. In most circumstances the sight is no more than a hint and most often that hint is the movement. This is best

Stalking too quickly.

observed from a stationary position. A moving observer has a different perspective of the environment and the faster the movement the more that perspective is changed.

2. Because trout's eyes are keenly tuned to detect movement we should progress accordingly. Ideally, stalking out of the fish's line of vision would be most successful, i.e., in his blind zone — but this is rarely possible. Therefore, because we are usually in sight we must use the knowledge that low relative movement is more difficult to see than fast movement (especially in blending tones).

Stalking slowly.

Effective stalking requires unrelenting and total concentration. This is more easily maintained if success is a frequent reward. It makes sense therefore to concentrate the greatest effort and stealth on those sections of a river where fish are more likely to feed. To linger too long in less favourable locations, without seeing movement, line or fin, leads to other attractions which may diminish concentration. Almost inevitably the next feeding trout is scared by a clumsy angler.

The suggestion, then, is that progress up a river is not a steady movement but a hasty passing of turbulent rapids or broad stony shallows leading to a slow deliberate sneak along a rocky reach or up to the eye of a pool. But never stop looking because the trout has a marvellous capacity to surprise. Expect to find it anywhere. With trout we can only talk of greater or lesser possibilities. By passing areas of lesser possibility quickly we are effectively increasing the proportion of fishing time in productive water.

A stalking angler should stop often. This necessity is illustrated by the following experience.

Two friends and I were making our way up the crystal-clear Leslie River. Without stopping we passed several deep pools, looking carefully as we went. Stands of leafy beech offered shade and concealment. In a half mile or river not one trout was seen. It couldn't be true. There had to be fish there. The bright conditions and overhead sun augmented our vision into the next pool so we stopped for a last inspection. Our immediate assumption was that there were no trout there either — but then the truth began to unfold! One shape became obvious, then another and another. Trout had been present all of the time but our haste had reduced our ability to see.

The weather can also affect the way we stalk and the speed of movement. The best day for stalking is a fine, calm one. In the bright sunlight and with little or no surface disturbance of the water, trout are easiest to see. Hence at times it is possible to stalk more quickly. Do not forget, though, that on such days the trout may more easily see you!

When clouds hide the sun, or wind and rain ruffle the water, a stalking angler has a far more difficult task. It is time then to alter stalking strategy.

There was a time when, if a strong wind was blowing or blustery showers swept the river, I would not go fishing or I would employ 'chuck 'n chance' methods. But I have since learned that such negative behaviour is not necessary. The conditions enforce a lowering of expectation but it is always possible to find a feeding trout somewhere.

Because fish are harder to see on a windy day or in the rain it is therefore essential to stalk even more slowly than usual, and search water in a close radius. There are two advantages thus given to the angler. His slower movement means he is less apparent to the fish and so he can get closer to his foes. In the poorer light it may be difficult to see fish but likewise it is harder for the trout to see the angler, again allowing closer contact.

It is a common belief among fishermen that fishing is not as good in wet or squally conditions. It is true that fewer fish are caught but is it not also true that fewer anglers try their luck? Such times are probably less conducive to insect hatches on the water but they do not prevent activity altogether. Terrestrial insects are shaken from trees and blown about, while life beneath the water surface continues to move.

I have seen proof of this many times. One of the most outstanding examples took place in the middle of May. Stories of spawning trout and salmon in the Hakataramea Stream attracted my interest and led me down to the river to observe.

*1. The mouth gives an indication
of the size of this brown trout.*

*2a. Graeme Marshall, fishing to
a good brown in gin clear water.*

2b. Another good fish about to be beached.

*5. In an almost primeval spot,
thick native bush down to the
stream, clear water, big fish.*

*6a. Drifting a nymph past the
fish's nose.*

6b. Walk slowly when spotting
trout.

8a. *A huge fish just cruising by.*
Disdaining our offerings he's still
there.

8b. Back country rivers require some effort to get to. A pause at the top of a hill on the way in.

*9a. The magic of evening as the
sun goes down.*

Wispy grey clouds descended quickly from the surrounding mountains and into the valley as I made my way upstream along tussocky banks. The forecast of snow to 300 metres became reality as I reached a long deep pool. Almost as if triggered by the flurry of snow flakes several large trout appeared at the water's surface and began sipping eagerly. Further upstream the same activity continued. It was a stimulating sight but a frustrating one too because the season had closed two weeks earlier.

Another time saw me insanely stalking up a rocky reach of the Mokihinui River in typical West Coast rain. My chances of spotting trout were marginal but that was sufficient to lure me to the water's edge. In these circumstances I moved particularly slowly and observed the water just in front of me. In addition only very likely lies received attention. There were obviously some insects about because a shape appeared nosing the surface a mere four metres ahead.

Keeping a Red Tipped Governor dry as I tied it to my nylon was no easy task in the heavy rain. The use of fly float solution is not one of my normal practices but false casting would not serve its drying function in the conditions, so this operation was undertaken, proving equally awkward. All the trouble was worthwhile and forgotten in moments as my fly was taken on the first offering. One furious run out into deep water, then a lunge straight down a bouldery rapid was the only contact I had with that fish. Thus, another tale of one that got away was born.

The next fish, which likewise fed on surface insects amid splattering rain droplets, showed avid interest in a delicately dropped fly. An initial flurry preceded a dogged battle but this time hook and line held. The magnificent 3.5 kg speckled brown which slid up the sandy beach was quickly released. Liberating such a fine creature gave immense satisfaction: a feeling second only to that of the take.

After another fat henfish had been deceived the wet and cold became intolerably uncomfortable and I returned to the refuge of the bush hut where my brother and friends lay snug in their sleeping bags. My entry through the hut door took their attention from reading, and the removal of layers of saturated clothing received considerable mockery, but inwardly I smiled because I knew that in years to come I would remember that day — they wouldn't.

One difficulty arising from keeping the eyes constantly on the water when stalking is that foot placement is usually by feel: a particularly difficult operation especially over rocks. No matter how an angler makes his way along a river bank, by feel (as I do) or by risking a loss in concentration to see the way, he must endeavour to tread as softly as possible. Heavy feet knocking rocks together send signals amazingly rapidly to trout many metres away. Fishermen may talk as loud as they wish because the air and water are two distinct mediums separated by the reflective surface film. The river bank and bed, however, are connected directly, with no buffer. Sounds and vibrations are readily transmitted to the water and have an electrifying effect on trout.

Windy Or Partly Cloudy Days

Two frustrating weather conditions to stalk in are when it is windy or when there are intermittent periods of sunshine and shade caused by a partly cloudy sky. While the wind gusts ruffle the water or when shade takes the place of sunlight it is most difficult to see. One tactic which can be employed to ease the frustration is to use the less favourable time to seek very likely lies — the eye of a pool for example. Then wait, where the water can be observed best, for either the wind gust to abate or the sunlight to appear. The result is that a lot of water will be passed untouched but the method makes best use of already diminished chances.

Body Movements

When a feeding trout has been sighted it is an exciting moment, a moment when anglers in their enthusiasm can easily lower their defences. So frequently I observe a trout's position being pointed out to a companion with a waving rod tip or extended arm. Furthermore the actions are made in haste.

Standing absolutely still is the safest way to look for trout. If movement of legs, arms, hands or head must be made then very slowly is best.

Rod carried in front.

The fishing rod could be considered an extension of an angler's body. It should always be carried behind and low when walking along a river bank, and never out over the water, in front, or vertically like an aerial. In that position it is only useful for waving goodbye to trout!

Where To Walk

Two things should be considered by a stalking angler when he is deciding on his best line of attack.

As stalking is a pointless exercise if the angler cannot see into the water, his initial concern is to adopt a line which gives the greatest advantage in this respect. The course though must allow utmost discretion because spotting trout which also spot you leaves little satisfaction and no fish in the creel.

Ideally a fisherman should stalk as low as possible, which of course means walking at water level. In addition, maximum use of the trout's blind zone must be made. Wading in the river is the only way of ensuring that we are in the blind zone but the disadvantages as a result

Stalking low.

(knocking stones together, sending tell-tale waves ahead, unnecessarily disturbing nymph habitat) far outweigh any gains.

A close look at the diagramatic representation of a trout's blind zone (figure 5) shows that as the distance increases behind a fish the wider the zone spreads. The importance of this is that we can safely stalk from the bank and remain in the blind zone if we scan water a reasonable distance ahead.

Many situations are less than ideal and from river level it is not always possible to see into the water far enough ahead. But if a little elevation is gained, unwelcome glare is reduced and stalking possible.

Two difficulties must be borne in mind when stalking from an elevated position. The trout's blind zone extends out behind but remember it is only effective near to the water's surface. A trout can see perfectly well anything which is elevated behind it. Also the higher a person stands the greater the chances of becoming silhouetted against the skyline. If you can climb higher yet avoid the silhouette problem, then a great advantage is gained.

Use Available Cover

Viewing a river from a bank which stands several feet high often provides excellent visibility a safe distance ahead. Frequently such banks are dotted with bushes and trees. The cover offered by vegetation should be used intelligently. By remaining behind a tree or bush a fisherman can see all he wishes in complete concealment. Care should be taken not to move branches unnecessarily. Trout react to any abnormality on the bank.

When bushes are only sparsely spread along the bank a fisherman may have to adopt an irregular path to remain in hiding. The river can

Photo 30
Use all available cover.

Photo 31 Photo 32
Walk back from edge on a
barren bank.

be safely approached from behind a bush. After reconnaissance is complete the bank should not be followed but walked away from at right angles (the way in) until out of view from the water's edge. It is then possible to move quietly upstream to the next cover which is approached in the same manner.

On other occasions a fisherman may be confronted by a barren bank. To negotiate along the edge would offer a welcome view to the trout. Here, one could try walking parallel to the edge but a few metres back. Thus the only part of the body exposed on the skyline is the head. Very slow movement is vital.

Unnatural foliage
movement.

Rear Cover

Being hidden by bushes in front is the ideal concealment for an angler, but standing still or walking deliberately, with cover behind, especially if it is nearby, is surprisingly good too.

I discovered this at the age of twelve. In those days I fished with fresh smelt or inanga on the Lower Clutha. The trout, which slashed among shoals of migrating smelt, usually occupied an edge territory which they patrolled constantly. They would make their way upstream, in clear view and within inches of the bank, to the top of their beat and then disappear out into the depths and obviously swim quickly downstream to appear at the lower part of the beat ready to begin again.

In attacking shoals of small fish they often killed or savaged many in a short time. They were not all devoured at once. Some were left drifting or writhing. These were plucked up at the trout's leisure when the frantic shoal had passed.

Stalking these fish was incredibly exciting for a twelve-year-old boy. I would watch the fish on its beat for a long time and calculate its pattern. When the trout disappeared on the downstream journey, out of sight, I would creep to the water's edge and lie as low as possible. Sometimes I could remain behind a tree but often I would be lying in full view but up against a bank or tree. Surprisingly the fish would swim to within a rod's length and as long as I remained still they would be undisturbed. The trick then was to lower my baited hook in line with the unsuspecting fish's beat, and wait! Those next few moments seemed a nerve-wracking eternity.

Use Shade As Cover

Looking into shaded waters is considerably more difficult than searching the depths of a nearby sunlit place. From the trout's viewpoint the situation is similar. When an angler steps into sunlight fish will scatter immediately, but by using any available shade an angler increases his camouflage immensely. If a choice exists, then use shade whether stalking or actually casting to a sighted fish.

Some Considerations Of Light

All objects we view in water or outside are made visible by the light they reflect or transmit. The greater the incoming light from the sun then the more distinct the image. Theoretically, then, the best conditions for viewing trout should be in bright sunlight. For a reasonable portion of the day and summer this holds true, but our ideal is complicated by the reflective nature of the surface of water.

If I had to choose, I would do most of my stalking in the middle of the fishing season (November to February) and in the middle of the day (9 a.m.-3 p.m.). The reason is that trout are easiest to see at these times.

In the middle of the day during high summer the sun travels high in the sky and the rays strike the water at approximately 90°. Con-

Photo 33
The effect of glare.

71

sequently most light is transmitted into the water illuminating all beneath. Furthermore, little is reflected from the water's surface to impair our vision.

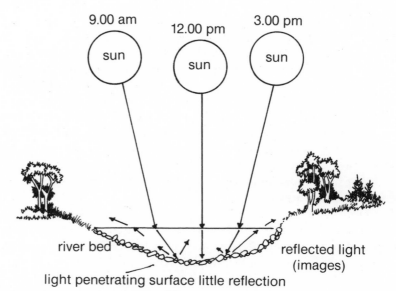

Illust 49
Sun high in summer —
most light penetrating
surface — little reflection.

light penetrating surface little reflection

Early or late in the day or near the end of the season the sun emits light from a lower angle. The result is that only part of the light is refracted through the surface to reveal what lies beneath. The rest is reflected as surface glare, the bane of a stalking angler.

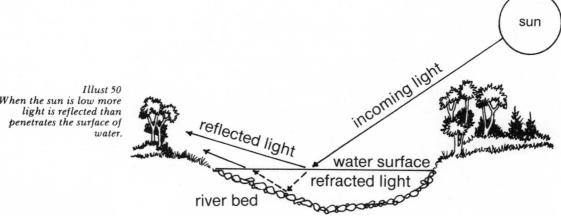

Illust 50
When the sun is low more
light is reflected than
penetrates the surface of
water.

Further difficulties for our problem-bound angler can eventuate even when the sun is not shining. On a partly cloudy day skies are bright as is the majority of the land. So, when the sun is not shining into the water and assisting the angler, a glare is still produced from the reflection of bright surrounds.

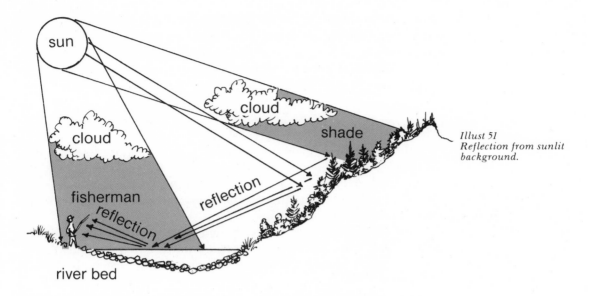

On cloudy days, land and vegetation near to a river or hillsides beyond are comparatively dark yet the sky surprisingly bright. A stalking angler facing a low horizon is therefore again confronted by acute angle reflection or glare.

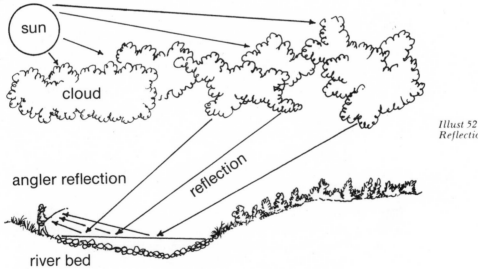

Illust 52
Reflection from cloud.

Some Strategies In Reducing Glare

When glare cannot be overcome an almost impossible task confronts us. But rarely does the situation arise where some action cannot be taken to improve vision.

Whether light is favourable or not the first aid to a fisherman is the use of polaroid glasses. Although they do not filter all reflected light they do reduce it considerably. Their effectiveness can be enhanced by: 1. Rotating the lenses; 2. Raising and lowering the head; 3. Shifting the body position; 4. Keeping the lenses shaded. 1, 2 and 3 all effectively diminish areas of reflected light which were not being reduced previously. The changes in position alter the angle or line of view.

Early And Late In The Day

With the sun rising in the easterly quarter in the morning, it is obvious that a stalking angler would be wise to fish, if possible, from the eastern bank (with the sun on his back). Later in the day, as the sun moved into the westerly quarter the opposite bank would possess the greatest advantage for spotting.

A question which could arise immediately is, which bank does an angler seek in the morning on a westward flowing river? Or conversely, how does a fisherman approach an eastward flowing stream in the late afternoon?

Using east and west banks is only hypothetical and a principle to bear in mind when planning. Rivers rarely flow exactly in one direction but twist and wind through most points of the compass in their quest for the sea.

Illust 53
Where to stalk in morning and afternoon on an easterly flowing stream.

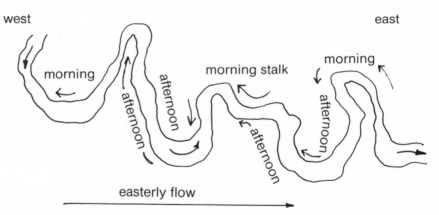

In narrow tree-lined valleys the reflection of sunlight from vegetation may be a more significant factor than direct sunlight itself. In such mountain streams the entire width of water is sunlit for only a brief period of the day. Before or after this time one side or other is shaded.

Recently I explored a delightful tributary of the Grey River. The day was perfect. There was no wind and not a cloud in the sky. The stream was small enough to allow a crossing below each pool. Tall beech trees reached out over both banks.

In the morning the eastern banks and edges lay in shade while the later afternoon saw shadows creeping and stretching over the western banks, and soon over the whole stream. Contrary to expectation, visibility into the water, at both times, was better with the sun in front. The reason was that when the sun was behind me it lit the trees on the opposite bank and this light was in turn reflected onto the water, producing glare. When I faced the sun I also faced tall shaded trees which provided a high backdrop and prevented unwanted reflections.

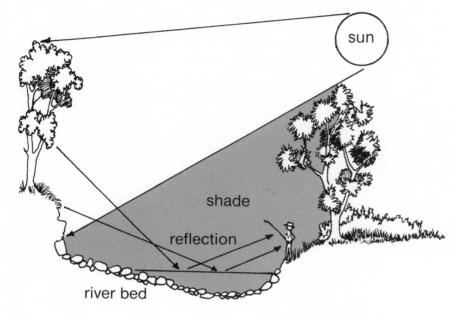

Illust 54
Reflection from sunlit trees ahead.

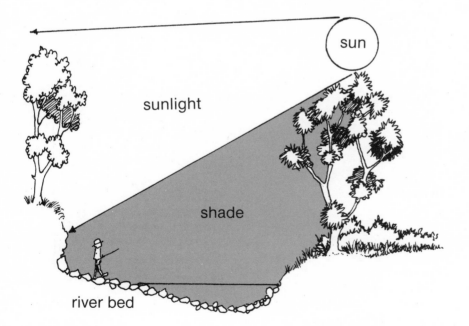

Illust 55
The advantage of a tall shady backdrop.

The Effect Of High And Low Horizons

Horizon height in front of an angler affects his vision enormously. The sky is usually brighter than all else and therefore the greatest source of unwanted glare. With a low horizon a greater proportion of sky is exposed offering maximum glare and an unfavourable angle of reflection to the angler.

Any strategy which can raise the horizon and reduce front light will improve visibility. One way of achieving this is to view the river from a more elevated position. Another is to use the opposite bank intelligently. River banks are commonly lined with trees. At times a fisherman will curse these as they present difficulties to his casting, but they can be a considerable aid in stalking. The area of a tree's reflection provides comparatively clear visibility into the water. An opposite bank lined with trees may raise the horizon as desired, particularly if the trees are tall and the stream narrow. High banks or cliffs on the other side of a stream give the same advantages.

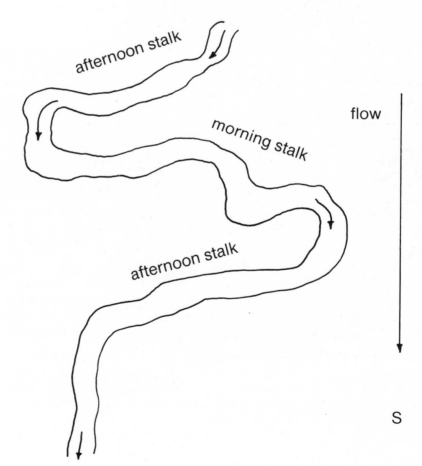

Illust 56
Where to stalk in morning and afternoon on a southerly flowing stream.

Concentration

Many anglers possess "the eye" to spot a good percentage of feeding fish — the fish being revealed by the factors previously outlined — yet the percentage they scare is also high. This failure is due to their mental approach.

Rarely is there any mention in conversation or literature regarding the psychology or mental approaches involved in trout fishing. The less tangible and more divergent nature of the subject probably accounts for our lack of interest. Nevertheless, I am inclined to think that a stalking angler's mental application and self-belief are as important as other skills in determining success.

In the last few years I have accompanied dozens of enthusiastic anglers (experienced and novices) in search of trout. They all demonstrated abundant enthusiasm as they stalked, in fact most were so keen that they underestimated or didn't fully understand the wary nature of their foe. The initial purpose in stalking trout is to spot a fish before it is alerted. To achieve this end, with a minimum of failures, necessitates unfailing concentration and single-mindedness. Most anglers seem to possess these qualities only for short periods of time.

Two anglers stalking together can complement each other and fish very successfully. Increase this number and expectations must drop. I have observed this frequently, but the most recent time is probably the easiest to recall.

Mid-December was a time of fickle weather in the Lewis Pass area. South-westerly fronts passed frequently and quickly, keeping rivers full although usually fishable. The Upper Grey proved uncrossable, so our party of four stalked together. Towering, stony cliffs provided an excellent backdrop and improved visibility into the sunlit waters ahead. One of the group inched his way forward as the spotter while the remainder lingered patiently a short distance behind, eager but restrained. The pool stretched for three hundred metres ahead, wide and gently rippling. Two hundred metres were passed and nothing seen: unexpected in such a delightful place. The eye of the pool was approached, then our spotter's patience was rewarded. He stopped and instinctively lowered his body. A smiling face, swivelled toward us, told what lay ahead.

Three of our rods remained tucked in their protective bags, so the one which had been threaded earlier was soon in action to complete the easier part of stalking. With a one hundred per cent record — one sighted, one caught — we resumed our stalk. Again a spotter took the lead and the others drifted behind, reflecting on the apparent scarcity of fish. Twenty more minutes of treading softly, rods behind and heads low, revealed the same. The local farmer had warned us to expect small numbers.

Halfway along an inviting bouldery reach a nose dimpled the water's surface, revealing a trout's presence. A second angler, half stumbling, half wading, positioned himself amid slippery, algae-covered rocks and began purposeful casting. The result was again positive. Not bad — two fish seen, two fish landed.

In at least 2 km of river we found just four feeding fish. Each was stalked with care and each was landed. Such success is rare in my experience. During the morning our approach had been very positive and our concentration unflagging. As the day wore on the approach changed. Of the four anglers, two were experienced and two relatively new to the sport. The novices, in their eagerness, quickened their pace, leaving the others behind. Any fish which may have been feeding was probably scared by a clumsy approach and inattention. I find it difficult to believe so much river could be as barren as our afternoon tally would suggest.

Do not misunderstand me. I am not trying to put down newcomers to angling, but merely endeavouring to highlight the need for intense concentration in stalking, particularly when trout are scarce. I scare more than my share of fish, and have chastised myself hundreds of times, but also recognise my failure as ineptitude, principally of the mind.

5

Fishing To Sighted Trout

One of the greatest thrills for me in fishing for trout is that electrifying moment when a feeding fish is spotted, especially if it is a large one, and still unaware of my presence. Few sights can reduce me to a shaking jelly so quickly.

Unfortunately, so many anglers blow it at this point by rushing things, and alarm the fish so that it flees from the clumsy angler or simply ceases feeding and lies doggo, aware that all is not well and ready to sprint for sanctuary at any moment.

Despite the excitement generated by the sighting of a veritable monster slurping large terrestrials off the surface or weaving from side to side in a fast run as it intercepts nymphs, the fisherman must let the initial excitement and nervousness subside before attempting to enter the fray. A sudden hasty movement or heavy footfall could make all the difference between a successful day and a totally blank one. Above all, the angler must be cool, calm and collected, and should be gathering in all the relevant data which would help weight the odds in his favour.

Once a fish is spotted, move quickly but with stealth. Excessive procrastination is not wise as trout are contrary creatures and could cease feeding quite without warning. If the fish is feeding actively, go to it. Be warned though – few of nature's creatures are as well endowed with survival equipment as rainbow and brown trout.

Let's consider some of the problems which beset the stalking angler once his intended prey has been spotted. We shall assume that the angler has carried out his stalking in a careful, methodical manner and that the trout has not been alarmed.

Angler's Spotting Position

Immediately the angler has spotted a fish he must consider the vulnerability of his own position in relation to the fish. Far too often the trout is not seen until the angler is virtually on top of it. The usual reaction of the fish is to cease feeding, then, as soon as the angler attempts to retreat into a casting position or cast a fly, to dash out into the centre of the river. This is an annoying experience, and one which is all too common, particularly on days when light conditions are poor for spotting. On a recent trip to the Wangapeka River I scared six fish in succession, despite the most careful and painstaking stalking. Light conditions precluded good stalking, and blind fishing was the only solution.

When a trout has been spotted by an angler, all too often the converse is true; the angler must make an immediate attempt to move from the fish's range of vision. Elevated positions are very dangerous in this regard and should be avoided unless plenty of cover is available. If possible use shade to hide in or simply keep a low profile. Once convinced that you have concealed your presence as much as possible, the next consideration is which fishing method to use.

Fishing Method And Gear

Again, method and observation is vital. Watch the fish closely. Is it taking nymphs or is it surface feeding? If the trout appears to be feeding sub-surface, then a nymph is probably the best choice. If feeding off the surface, then a dry fly is probably appropriate, though nymphing trout will often take a dry fly and vice versa.

Depth Of Water And Speed of Current

If the fish is feeding in deep (1m +) water, then a long leader is almost essential, and long means at least 3.5 m up to 5 m, or even more in extreme cases. Conversely, in very shallow water a leader of only 3 m or less will suffice as the fly will not need to be cast well above the feeding fish.

In deep, fast water the problem of presenting a nymph at the fish's level is exacerbated by drag operating on the flyline and leader. One solution is to cast the nymph well above the fish or to employ a tuck cast, one which stops the nymph abruptly well above the water surface and enables it to sink unhindered by the flyline. As the nymph strikes the surface of the water the rod is raised to take as much of the floating line off the surface as possible.

The value of this method was proved to me by fly fishing guide, Tony Entwistle of St Arnaud. We were fishing the wild, boisterous and beautiful Upper Buller one fine Sunday, when Tony spotted a trout nymphing in a deep pocket right under a swirl of white water. Tony offered me first go at it – a generous gesture as I had already been fishing the water blind in the lead. Try as I might I could not get my nymph past the trout at the correct level. Occasionally the fish would rise and make a half hearted attempt at taking. Eventually I gave up and offered Tony a go. He was using a much longer leader and using the tuck cast and lift to advantage, was able to induce a take on his second cast.

Since that time, some years ago, I have used the method successfully on some difficult fish.

Casting Position

One of the most vital factors in successful upstream fly fishing is choice of casting position. Obviously, river characteristics and other elements vary so markedly that hard and fast rules are inappropriate.

There are two schools of thought regarding upstream casting, and both have merit. They are: (a) the direct upstream cast and (b) the acute angle cast.

*Photo 35
Direct upstream
nymphing.*

The writers favour the former in most situations for a number of reasons, perhaps best illustrated by an actual incident.

Les was fishing the glorious Mataura in the vicinity of the gravel dredge when he noticed a number of trout rising boldly some metres out from the bank on a long, evenly flowing stretch. He decided to cast to the downstream fish from an oblique position. Time after time he presented the dry fly, seemingly perfectly. To an onlooker, no drag whatsoever was apparent. Although the fish showed no alarm, it simply refused every fly offered. Each fish was tried in turn with the same disappointing result. As a last resort, Les elected to try fishing directly upstream. The trout were still feeding happily so he quietly slipped in behind the last one and gently cast up the original fly. On the first drift past, the size 18 fly was quietly sucked in and the fish hooked. A few nearby fish were alarmed by the commotion and were put down, but others were fooled as well. Obviously despite careful line mending, some drag was still being detected by the fish. The upstream cast was eliminating most of the drag – at least enough to fool the fish.

Photo 36
Fishing upstream with a
dry fly.

There are many occasions when casting directly upstream is not practical or indeed, is impossible. One advantage of a cast made from an acute angle or from an almost right-angled position is that the fish is shown less of the leader. There is also less likelihood of the leader splashing down heavily on top of the fish, thereby alarming it.

A distinct disadvantage of the acute angle cast is that the fly is allowed only a very short drift before becoming influenced by the drag of the current. Skilful line mending can allow a longer drift, but as has been postulated earlier, even a degree of drag imperceptible to the angler may be enough to alarm a discerning trout, particularly one feeding off the surface.

A further problem when selecting a casting position is the tendency of many anglers to enter the water far too close to the fish. I have observed trout to go rigid immediately an angler slips into the water in an attempt to get in behind it. Often this is caused by a stone being dislodged, but must also be caused by the vibrations set up both in the water and through the stream bed. The best advice is, always enter the water well below the optimum casting position and then, if necessary, move carefully into the chosen spot.

In many situations the directly upstream casting position is probably the best as it enables the angler to use the sun to advantage. For instance, if one is forced to cast from a position to the left of a fish while the sun's rays are shining from the same angle, the chances are that line shadow will alarm the trout. From a directly downstream position the angler has a choice, not just relating to the angle of the sun, but also to wind direction and speed of current as well.

Speed And Variability Of Current

There are few situations where the current is truly laminar in flow. Variability of the stream bed and bends in the stream mean that many conflicting currents may exist in even one small part of a river. The problems to the stalking angler are many, and obviously solutions cannot be suggested for all of them here.

The nymph fisherman has additional difficulties in that he cannot readily ascertain what is happening below the surface. It is not unusual for a whole new set of currents to be operating just above the stream bed. In general though, currents are slower at the stream bed level than on the surface. Therefore the angler needs to keep good control over the line by stripping-in excess floating line. To maintain close contact with the floating line means that the angler is more easily able to detect a strike and take up slack when setting the hook. Some anglers also use good line control to advantage by employing an induced take technique such as the Leisenring lift which simulates a nymph rising from the stream bed to the surface.

Fly Placement

Correct, accurate fly placement on the first cast is often critical with well educated trout. The stalking angler should endeavour to place the fly in the optimum position with the minimum of disturbance.

I recall one highly frustrating day on the Motueka River a few summers ago. The day was superb with not a cloud in a sky of deepest blue. The river was showing the effects of no appreciable rain in the preceding two weeks and was very low and clear. Somewhat strangely the willows hung limp in the blazing sun as the normal sea breeze chose not to blow on this occasion. One would have expected the trout to be skulking in the deep holes and under shady willows. Not so. Trout stood out on the wide, shingle runs and shallow glides. They were everywhere. In fact, in one long run I counted over forty. I couldn't believe my luck, especially when it became obvious that they were feeding well too. Dimple rises punctuated the surface and other fish could be observed weaving from side to side taking nymphs.

To cut a long story short, I returned home despondent and fishless that day. The reason? Besides the obvious fact that the trout could in all probability see me as easily as I could them, I put down my striking lack of success to poor casting and fly placement. In retrospect I realised that I was showing each fish far too much leader and I was indulging in excessive false casting over the fish. Admittedly, the very low, flat water and lack of breeze didn't help, but I did a bit of soul searching after being taken to the cleaners so comprehensively.

I now measure casting distance to a fish by avoiding false casting *over* the fish. Wherever possible I place a cast or two directly out at right angles from my casting position and then place the fly on the water with only one or two false casts at most. Ideally no false casts should go over the fish and the cast should never splash the water behind the fish. If an error is made though the cast should be fished out and not whipped off the water immediately.

Striking

The term "striking" is in some ways a misnomer in that the fly fisherman rarely has to lift the rod very quickly. Often all that is required is a lift of the rod until the fish is felt. However, when a lot of line is on the water it is sometimes necessary to strike hard in order to take up the slack. When dealing with striking it must be stated categorically that every fish is different, and must be treated as an individual case. One general rule which may be applied to both nymph and dry fly fishing is that the faster the water the quicker the strike should be. There are very significant differences between striking on dry fly and nymph. While generally regarded as the most difficult form of fly fishing for trout, dry fly fishing will be dealt with first as it is easier to see just what is happening.

Photo 37
The 'strike'.

Dry Fly:

Striking on a trout which has taken a dry fly must be slow except perhaps in the very fastest water. It must be understood that the trout takes a dry fly into its mouth with quite a quantity of water. If the strike is too soon the hook does not even have a chance of taking hold. One of the greatest dilemmas faced by a fly fisherman is that of deciding just when to strike. We have devised a general rule which seems to work quite well, and that is to wait until the fish has turned down and settled after taking the fly. Still, I find that it is not unusual for the strike to meet with absolutely no resistance whatsoever, despite careful timing. This may be caused by very stiff hackles holding the hook away from the inside of the fish's mouth. When a trout is missed on the strike with a nymph, the hook can sometimes be felt scraping across the inside of the mouth, but just failing to take hold. The most experienced of anglers miss fish on the strike or simply prick them. This is an inevitability which the most careful timing and sharpest hooks will not prevent.

Nymph:

Striking with the nymph usually needs to be more of a reflex action than with dry fly. It does not necessarily need to be as fast as some angling scribes would have us believe. In fact, in very slow water such as in backwaters, the trout is very deliberate about picking up and taking in the nymph.

Striking too soon simply takes it from the fish before the hook has time to gain a purchase.

Contrary to popular belief, trout do quite frequently hook themselves with a nymph. This sometimes happens in fast water when drag on the floating line is sufficient to set the hook with little or no effort from the angler. Normally though, the fisherman must set the hook by raising the rod tip and stripping in line with the free hand.

Nymph takes can be indicated to the angler in two ways. The first is when the angler actually sees the fish move to where he assumes the nymph to be. In most cases the take is a deliberate movement, usually sideways and often upwards in order to take a nymph passing above the fish. Experience is the only teacher when detecting nymph takes. The experienced nymph angler knows almost instinctively when the trout has taken the artificial in preference to a natural. On some occasions though the take is not observed as the artificial is taken by the fish without moving at all. Other indications that the nymph has been taken include a roll in the water and flash of white belly — even a glimpse of white inside the trout's mouth.

Many fishermen rely entirely on their floating line to indicate a strike, and this is a very reliable method. In discoloured or disturbed water the actual take can be difficult to discern. This is when a strike indicator is very useful. When fishing blind, an indicator of some brightly coloured material is almost essential unless one is using a highly visible floating line. I find that a small piece of red wool attached to the leader where it joins the floating line works well.

The angler must get into the habit of striking every time the line hesitates or stops. Sometimes the take is very gentle, just enough to slow the line. When in doubt strike, as no time must be lost. When the line stops the fish has well and truly taken the nymph and will eject it quickly if allowed to. Good line control is vital to avoid excessive line precluding a good hook-up. Interestingly I find that I rarely miss a fish on the strike when using the line as an indicator. Personally, on a percentage basis I miss fewer fish on nymph than on dry fly.

As experience is gained and instincts honed, one misses fewer and fewer fish on the strike. I've had some amazingly frustrating days though. I recall a day on the Travers in Nelson Lakes National Park when I struck on eight separate fish with dry fly and nymph. Some were missed on the strike and others came off on the first run. Les, on the other hand, hooked eight and landed six beautiful fish. Such is life. I have to admit to an almost overwhelming urge to smash my rod into little pieces, throw it into the river then leap in after it. In retrospect the day was quite amusing. It was anything but funny at the time though!

Strategies For Specific Lies

(a) The Eye of a Pool.

The importance of this particular lie has been stressed earlier. While fish are often quite easy to spot in this position, some problems can be posed by swirling currents. Where the eye is formed as the river makes a major turn in direction, a back eddy frequently occurs at the bottom of the eye. Fish will sometimes be found facing 'downstream', necessitating a careful approach.

Most 'eye'-dwelling fish are actively feeding on items of food being swept past in the current, while actually lying on the bank side of the very distinct line of delineation between fast and slow water. The fish expects to have to intercept food being swept past in the faster water, so it is to the faster water that the initial cast at least should be made. This line of delineation is normally almost laminar in flow, so that drag is minimised. Fish feeding from this very fast water often take surprisingly quickly, and the angler needs to be ready for a sharp turn sideways, especially when fishing the nymph, as the trout can intercept and reject the artificial with amazing speed.

The cast should be made to land the nymph about a metre above the fish. Obviously though, if the trout is lying in deep water, say more than 70 cm, the cast will need to be further up to allow the nymph to sink. One of the most common faults made by anglers is to 'line' the fish by casting too far above it. In most conditions any hint of floating line in the trout's window will bring about a rapid departure. The best insurance against lining the fish is to use long leaders of at least three to four metres.

If casts into the fast water fail to elicit a response, the other side may be tried. Sometimes the current is just too fast for the fish to devour one's fly, no matter how appetising. A drift through the quieter part of the eye does sometimes work, especially with a drag-free dry fly imitating a large terrestrial such as a beetle or spider.

(b) Tail of Pool.

In my experience trout are normally hard to take in this area unless there are riffles and pockets just above the line where the water begins to spill into the next pool or run.

Normally the angler casting to fish observed in this area is faced by the problem of increasing current velocity as the stream runs towards the tail. This increase in speed tends to create serious drag problems, exacerbated by the surface smoothness which enables the fish to see angler and line. One way of avoiding drag is to approach as close as possible and use only a short line. This method requires great stealth and a low, crouching approach. Another is to deliberately 'snake' cast. This allows the fly more natural drift before being accelerated by the current.

(c) Front of Rock.

A problem, frequently found in fast-moving back country streams especially, is the fish which likes to lie on the upstream side of a large rock or other obstruction. After experiencing many failures by trying to

*Trout
in front of a rock*

cast around the side of the obstruction, one day it suddenly dawned on me that the reason for the trout's refusal was the old enemy, drag. I realised that the trout was lying in an almost current-free zone and was very reluctant to venture out of this to feed. Casts around the side of the obstruction were causing the fly to be unceremoniously dragged out of the very limited feeding zone.

Casting over a rock to avoid drag.

GRANTWINTER.

A cast over the top was the only solution. Since realising this I've had a high success rate with such fish by dropping a short accurately-cast fly almost right on the trout's nose, even if the rock or obstruction is quite a way out of the water. Try it next time you are faced with a similar problem.

(d) Lee of Rock.

Contrary to popular opinion, trout using the area behind a large obstruction like a rock are rarely found very close to it. Observation will show that this area is often very disturbed, allowing little quiet water for a trout to rest in. Most fish will be found some metres back downstream in an area of quiet, largely laminar flow.

Like fish using the eye of a pool, most of the food is extracted from the faster water to the side of the fish. Hence the first cast should always be to the side along the line of delineation between faster and slower water. One advantage to the angler of this position is that the sun can be allowed for, so that if the sun is shining from the right side, the cast can be made to the left, eliminating the line shadow, and vice versa.

(e) The Lee of a Bank Extension.

While the pocket formed is often considerably narrower than a true eye at the head of a run or pool, this can be a prime spot and one

Photo 38
Fishing to water in lee of
bank extension.

relatively easy to fish, as the trout will normally be holding very close to the bank and in laminar current flow.

As for the eye, the area to be fished first should always be down the line dividing faster and slower water.

This particular lie is more likely to hold fish early in the season in my experience. I suspect that these fish are relatively easily caught and consequently don't remain there long, or they seek safer water as the season progresses. There is a greater likelihood of fish holding here throughout the season if the water is relatively deep and if cover in the form of streamside foliage or undercut banks is present.

(f) Fishing to a Fish which is Not Visible from the Casting Position.

Clive (Chappie) Chapman is a fanatical and highly skilled angler who has very few blank days. However, he recounted a very frustrating experience once which has stuck in my memory.

He had fished the Matiri River in the Murchison area without success one day and was just about to begin the long downstream plod back to the car when he decided to have a look at one more pool. In best Red Indian style he crawled to the edge of a fine looking pool where he carefully viewed the water from an elevated position. As he cautiously parted the scrub his heart missed a beat or two as he spied a very large trout. Now Chappie is no more inclined to exaggerate than I, so I had to believe him when he claimed that the fish was at least 5 kg and probably nearer 6!

Carefully he marked the position then crawled back downstream some distance before moving up to a casting position. To his dismay, though, at river level the water was impossible to see into, even with polaroids and peaked hat, because of the low angle of the sun.

He moved gently back up to the high bank. Sure enough the leviathan was still there. Yet again he attempted to get into a casting position. Again, he was thwarted as the whole scene changed at river level.

Eventually he attempted to mark the fish's position by relating it to prominent features on the bank. He never did hook the fish despite a number of extra careful casts. When he went back to the observation point yet again, the fish had disappeared, probably put down by a slightly over long cast.

This incident illustrates the value of a fishing companion. Though I love fishing alone, a mate to share the joys and heartbreaks is best of all, especially as it can actually mean putting more fish in the bag. Obviously, Chappie would have been in a much better position if he had a second pair of eyes spotting for him from the high bank.

Nonetheless, the solitary angler can get by if he applies a few basic rules. Without a doubt the most important qualities are concentration and a positive attitude, particularly important to the angler who fishes alone on a dull day.

Many fish are spotted from elevated positions but are impossible to see at river level. The angler must get into the habit of relating the fish's position to other nearby features. In fact, time should be spent memorising the exact position, not just in relation to one feature, but a number of them. This is where careful fly selection and the first cast are vital. I have successfully landed many fish by applying this approach.

Little things are often of great importance in trout fishing and, to conclude, I propose to summarise a few of them:-

(a) Always maintain concentration.

(b) Tread quietly and move with slow, considered movements.

(c) Don't wander along with the rod held out in front.

(d) Use long leaders and try to avoid drag.

(e) Consider the position of the sun.

(f) If a fish is difficult to see at river level, memorise its position.

Two anglers working together.

6

The Backcountry Experience

What the Americans term 'back-packing' for trout has really caught on in this country. As long as trout have existed in the headwaters of remote New Zealand rivers there have been fishermen keen to catch them. The tramper/angler or hunter/angler has long been a part of the New Zealand scene, but the upsurge in interest in back country fishing for fishing's sake in the last ten years is nothing short of phenomenal. While the implications of this in terms of conserving the resource are discussed elsewhere in this publication, it has to be stated that some members of the angling fraternity look upon the increased pressure with a modicum of dismay and anxiety.

As I have argued elsewhere there needn't be conflict so long as back country anglers exercise restraint and responsibility. Sure, one is bound to see a few more fishermen on the river, and in some very unexpected places too, but these meetings should be mutually beneficial, with the dialogue and exchange of ideas helping both groups. I've met some great people in some of the strangest places at times, and only rarely have I had cause to feel anxious about the threat they posed to the fishery. Trout anglers as a group are a reflective, thinking breed, and those prepared to walk for days, totally self-contained, even more so.

What Is The Back Country Experience?

Obviously, perception of the back country fishing experience varies, though I feel that it is possible to find common denominators. Definition of what constitutes back country is difficult. I suppose that it could loosely be described as being difficult of access and well away from centres of population. Generally, we are dealing with the middle and upper reaches of a major river, as well as its tributaries. Back country immediately brings to mind steep, beech-clad hillsides rising to golden tussock tops, but this is not necessarily so, for many Canterbury, Otago and Southland back country rivers run through treeless terrain. No, the prime qualification is the relative remoteness of the area.

If trout en masse are the object, then one need go no further than Taupo or the Mataura. In fact, many first time back country anglers

93

are disappointed by the numbers of trout seen, especially in the upper reaches where good holding water becomes scarce.

The back country experience is much more than just fishing. It is also essentially a cleansing of the mind, and if I might be permitted to use so grandiloquent a term, a spiritual experience. I'm not a religious man in that I don't belong to any specific faith. Nonetheless, I challenge anyone to remain unaffected or unchanged in some way after a few days in the headwaters of a free-flowing, unspoiled wild river. Others with a more lyrical style can describe the spirit of these places far more vividly than I. One has only to read the final chapters of Norman Marsh's *Trout Stream Insects of New Zealand* to understand how a person can feel about his favourite chunk of wilderness. Many who share Norman's sentiments envy his descriptive gifts.

Yet another part of the total experience is simply surviving and living in relative comfort in an often hostile environment. There is a great sense of personal satisfaction to be gained from making one's way in the wilderness, away from the pursuit of the dollar and trappings of materialism. One of life's great pleasures is sitting back after a hearty campfire-cooked meal with a huge cup of tea, quietly discussing the day's events or the prospects of the next. I even enjoy tent or hut-bound days when the rain beats down and the trees thrash wildly in the wind. Such days are an unexpected luxury and afford the opportunity to doze, read a book and chat with one's companions. Frequent brews punctuate the day which passes almost too quickly sometimes, offering as they do a rare chance for total relaxation. Young children and a wife with lists of jobs to be done see to it that even Sundays and holidays are busy at home!

The pursuit of monster trout is most certainly the prize attraction of the up-country rivers. I really do dream of catching a trophy fit to grace the space above the fireplace. I wonder if it proves to be an anti-climax? Fortunately there is much more to such places than fishing, and even relatively unsuccessful trips are memorable for other reasons. As a keen deerstalker I'm always on the lookout for game, though the interest is largely academic as a rifle is rarely carried on our trips. I recall one brilliant early morning on the Karamea when I watched three red deer picking their way back and forth across a shingly beach. Their red summer coats were highlighted by early morning light to the extent that individual hairs on their backs could be picked out in silhouette. I marvelled, too, at their highly tuned senses. As I watched, three alert heads snapped up simultaneously, ears pricked. The lead hind wasted no time in covering the fifty metres to the sanctuary of the bush, followed closely by her younger brethren. Just as they were swallowed up by the foliage I too heard the drone of the Hughes 500 in the distance. Seconds later it swung around the bend in the river, the shooter, hanging half out of the doorless machine giving a cheery wave as the helicopter flashed overhead at treetop height. "One up to the deer," I murmured, grinning, as I continued on up to the river.

My knowledge of birdlife and of the bush generally has increased markedly in the last ten years or so. Where once I would spend virtually

Illust. 60
"Back packing" to back country waters.

every waking hour fishing, I'm just as apt these days to spend quite a bit of time wandering through an interesting patch of bush. Les Hill has become quite interested in ferns, and enjoys the challenge of trying to photograph them in natural light. I've certainly become more alert to changes in plant associations such as those brought about by altitude or change in aspect, and pleasurable time is spent trying to identify birds from their calls.

I recall vividly Les's first sighting of a kiwi in the wild. He was having a wash in a tiny creek at twilight after a long, hard day on the hoof when a strange creature stepped into the creek and boldly waded across, apparently unconcerned by the interloper. Les looked again and realised that he was face to face with his very first live kiwi. Strangely, it bore no resemblance to the 'Goodnight Kiwi' on the T.V. at all!

95

Not all the experiences on a back country fishing trip are pleasurable. I can recall some very difficult, even dangerous days of clambering around slippery bluffs and crossing potentially hazardous flooded rivers. The dangers are there and must not be taken lightly by any party. Possibly the most frightening experience I've had occurred some years ago in north-west Nelson. Our party of four was lounging around the remnants of the campfire and thinking about going to bed. The evening was just one out of the box — still, balmy and giving promise of another fine day to come, when without warning a huge dead standing kahikatea crashed to the ground, shattering into a hundred pieces only metres from our carefully chosen campsite. Not a word was spoken for some moments afterwards, and when it was wouldn't pass the publisher anyway so won't be repeated. Four very jittery, frightened boys crawled into their sleeping bags that night, and all had nightmares about what might have happened if the camp had been sited elsewhere.

Planning A Trip

Most of my trips are worked out twelve months in advance. I consider myself fortunate indeed to have the best fishing mates anyone could hope for, and 'Hill's Tours' as they are affectionately known, are highlights on this sportsman's calendar. Entry to 'the tour' is very strictly by invitation only, and newcomers are only allowed if approved by all established members. New chums have to serve an apprenticeship, and are normally held responsible for rousing the party with a brew in the morning. Suffice it to say that we have a lot of fun and share some of life's great experiences.

Along with the camaraderie, banter and near constant ribbing is a more serious side. Preparation is meticulous. Each party member is expected to be reasonably fit and in a state of health which should not prove a hindrance to others. Individuals are responsible for personal equipment, and group provisioning, including finance, is delegated to certain people.

Briefly, factors to be considered include the following: transport to the roadhead; food; tents; camping equipment; first aid and emergency supplies. Planning must be thorough. Failure to plan carefully could result in a poor diet, inadequate protection from the elements and consequent stress in the group.

Today's freeze-dried food is a credit to the manufacturers — e.g., sliced lamb and green peas — (the nearest thing to fresh lamb sliced off the Sunday roast I've tasted). Similarly, virtually all other meal essentials can now be found in a lightweight form. The exceptions, which we like to eat, are things like salami and cheese which we use as day time snacks, and also sugar. I recall days of 30 kg-plus packs and compare them to today's 20 kg maximum. It pays to shop around at the local supermarket.

Unless staying in huts, it is sensible to take a good tent and fly sheet.

Some people are now using large "super-flies" almost exclusively. These are terrific in that the extra bulk and weight of a tent is not carried — a great advantage if the group is only intending to camp out a few nights or if huts are full.

Primuses or various forms of portable stoves are great. In some areas firewood is scarce, making the inclusion of at least one portable cooker almost essential. We carry at least two and use them a lot, especially for the warming cup of hot soup after a long, cold day in the river.

First aid requirements are often overlooked by groups. In addition to

Photo 41
A typical back country trout.

personal kits, a group kit should be carried. A few essentials include burn cream, insect repellent and phenergan.

For details of equipment to carry on an extended trip into the hills the Mountain Safety Bushcraft Manual should be studied and a copy carried.

The Fishing

New Zealand is blessed by having dozens of free-flowing rivers in each island. They all have their origins in natural high country areas. Most are relatively short, and many have rather low numbers of wild, self-supporting brown and rainbow trout. It is not unusual for some trout in these streams to grow to prodigious sizes and every year many fish in excess of 4.5 kg are taken. The high average size and the ever-present possibility of catching a trophy fish, coupled with the beautiful surroundings, combine to draw more and more anglers every year.

The rivers, by their very nature, limit the population density. Rather than producing big numbers, these streams produce big fish. There is simply not the food or holding water to sustain large numbers of small trout. Until man comes along to upset it these populations are essentially in balance with their environment, which no amount of stocking would alter.

Many of these large up-river dwellers become very possessive about their territory, and if they are not 'sole occupiers' of an entire pool or run, then they soon see to it that they command the best feeding position by instituting a hierarchy, or pecking order. Close study of a pool containing a number of feeding trout soon leaves little doubt as to who is boss fish. He or she will hold the prime lie and defend it vigorously if need be if smaller fry are presumptuous enough to try their luck.

These 'top fish' are the prey of the thinking angler. However, being

Photo 42
A constant back country hazard.

aggressive does not necessarily mean that they are easy meat for the angler — far from it. These very big fish are also big in the commonsense department too. That's how they attained their size!

Many people new to back country fishing think that because such fish rarely see human beings they are less likely to spook than their heavily fished low country cousins. Nothing could be further from the truth. Last season my good friend, Brian Smith, and I were fishing the headwaters of a Westland river. I was able to look into a large pool off a high bluff. There was plenty of vegetation so being seen wasn't a problem. Smithy was on the opposite bank and approaching the pool cautiously when I spotted a huge fish, which I would estimate at being in the 5 kg class, lying just on the downstream side of a prominent lip running diagonally across the pool.

Photo 43
Typical back country
water.

The trout was nymphing freely and looked a sitter, and I directed Smithy into a casting position. He dropped to one knee and expertly cast up into the fast water above the lip. I expected to see a capacious mouth open and suck in the nymph, as the cast appeared to be as near perfect as possible. Instead, the fish went rigid. Smithy tried again. This time the fish didn't hesitate and slowly but surely sank like a submarine into the blue-green depths of the pool and was soon lost to sight.

What went wrong? The approach was low and the line cast no shadow. I'm certain that neither of us had been spotted, and the fish had not been lined. Eventually we decided that the diagonal nature of the lip had caused an almost imperceptible amount of drag on the fly. This is what the back country angler is up against — extremely wary creatures in an environment with which they are totally familiar. The odds are very much on the side of the fish much of the time. Don't despair, though, as they *can* be caught. How? By applying the principles already outlined in this book. Unless spin fishing or blind nymphing in discoloured water, the stalking back country angler will be attempting to spot his prey. With this in mind there is little point in starting to fish early in the morning, whatever many books say. The low angle of the sun poses two problems: (1) It is very difficult to see into the water because of the reflection, and (2) the line casts a shadow guaranteed to put any fish down.

Nine a.m. is early enough and gives the angler until about six or seven in the evening before the same problems occur at the other end of the day. I've always preferred fishing between 9 a.m. and 3 p.m. After that the light does not seem quite so good, and the problems are further compounded by the almost inevitable cloud build-up in spring and early summer, as well as the often quite savage wind which gets up in the early afternoon.

However, on the other side of the coin, the afternoon breeze can be a blessing by disguising the line hitting the water. It can also allow one to approach less cautiously. The afternoon hours seem to be better for the dry fly too. I swear by large terrestrial imitations at this time of day, and in fact even if a fish is not rising I'll try it first with a size 10 Molefly or Red Tipped Governor. Both patterns can be deadly in the middle of a hot summer afternoon when the trout are looking for large beetles or cicadas. The blood pressure rises something awful when a 3 kg jack opens a mouth big enough to admit a beer can as it wolfs down a high floating Molefly!

The Molefly is the only dry pattern I will fish blind in very broken or pocket water, when fish are not easy to spot. On a large river like the Karamea this method sometimes works well, and usually provides some surprises.

At times of normal flow most New Zealand back country streams are amazingly clear. Overseas visitors have often seen nothing quite like them and rave about being about being able to see every pebble on the bottom. In these conditions long leaders are the only way to go. Most anglers can handle a 5 m leader if it is constructed correctly from both

*Photo 44
A Forest Service hut
commonly used by back
country anglers.*

hard and soft monofilament. I do not subscribe to the highly scientifi-
cally designed and balanced tapered leaders so commonly described in
overseas books and magazines. As long as 60-70% (the butt section) is
made up of hard monofilament and the rest of soft, there are usually
not too many problems with casting. If tying one's own leaders, it is
important that it tapers gradually. For instance, a 12 kg b.s. butt
section should not then be joined directly to a 2 or 3 kg section. I find
that the longer the leader the greater the need there is to start the butt
section with the heaviest practicable nylon. In the back country I

rarely go below 2.7 kg b.s. tippets. Anything less than this and you are likely to get egg on your face. It's amazing how often what appears to be a 2 kg fish is in reality 3 kg or more. Back country fish are often very short, deep and powerful.

In December 1982 I caught and released such a fish — one I was convinced was around the 2 kg mark. When it finally flopped on its side in the shallows I realised that I had been connected to a fish of around 4 kg.

The need to employ great stealth cannot be over-emphasised, but one's greatest asset in the back country is a good companion, not only for safety reasons but also to help spot fish. By virtue of their mountainous, high country location, these streams are prone to high rainfalls and a high percentage of rainy or cloudy days. When really torrential rain is falling rivers rise quickly, but miraculously drop again quickly almost as soon as the downpour stops. Really flooded rivers are unfishable, but with the help of a companion, trout can be caught by normal methods on grey days and in equally grey rivers.

Working as a team and fishing to alternative fish works well with the non-angler guiding each cast. Inclement conditions can mean one often has to be almost right on top of a fish before being able to spot it. Where the stream permits, we spot for each other from behind any available cover and from above river level. Guiding of this nature has definitely brightened up some dull days where a solitary angler would be struggling even to place the fly correctly, let alone see a nymph take.

Steep valley sides have their advantages too. On grey days positioning oneself opposite a steep bank or line of tall trees can improve the success rate greatly by allowing one's eyes to penetrate the surface sheen. Conversely, on a bright day the shadow cast by a tree or bank is almost impossible to see into.

Back Country Fly Patterns

Just like the perennial arguments in mountain huts over 'the best' rifle calibre, so too do opinions vary on trout flies. If I really had the courage of my convictions I would head for the hills with only one dry fly pattern and one nymph pattern in my possession. I'm convinced that the actual pattern is not particularly important, but size and weight is. If I was limited to only one of each, my preference would be for Molefly dries, in sizes 14-10 and for Pheasant Tail nymphs in sizes 16-10. Then again, just to make sure, I would probably toss in a few Green Beetles and Red Tipped Governors as well as a Kakahi Queen or two. A few large stonefly nymphs along with some Hare and Coppers and Halfbacks, not to mention a few March Browns, would not go amiss. The list could go on and on, but in all seriousness I believe that the first mentioned would suffice.

My fly tying ability, or lack of it, is well known to my angling companions. In fact, I must confess to a certain lack of expertise in this field. Nonetheless I have persevered over the last five or six years and feel quite pleased with some of my recent nymph ties.

Over a period of about four years I have worked at developing a good, general pattern for back country use, and last summer I believe I finally proved the worth of one particular pattern which met with very few refusals indeed. It is now used with confidence on back country streams, and also at times when lower country streams are flowing at a higher than normal level. Just to bring me down to earth though, it proves singularly uninteresting to trout in the height of mid-summer and in low, clear water. Perhaps they can examine the pattern at their leisure and are less likely to be taken in by the deception.

While loosely based on a pheasant tail shape, the M.M. (Marshall's Monstrosity) was not tied with any particular branch of the family ephemeroptera in mind. However, using the super-normal releaser theory I attempted to highlight particular areas of the insect anatomy at the time of emergence.

My most recent version of the nymph, and there is guarantee that it will not change again, is tied in sizes ranging from 16-10. All are tied with some extra weight — some only lightly with a little copper wire, and others with fairly large amounts of lead wire for use in very fast or deeper than normal pools and runs. In my experience few commercially tied nymphs have anywhere near enough weight in them. Nymphing trout feed largely on, or near, the stream bed so imitations must be capable of getting down to that particular level.

The M.M. Nymph:-

Hook: 10-16
Thread: Black or Olive
Thorax: Dark brown or reddish possum fur
Abdomen: Green seal fur
Wing Case: Peacock herl
Legs: Optional, or brown hen hackle
Tails: Golden pheasant tail tippets

Tying Method:

Take tying thread to the tail and tie in tail fibres. Wrap fine copper wire or lead wire around the hook and form a plump thorax. Wind thread back behind thorax and tie in peacock herl. Wind thread back to the tail and dub finely chopped seal's fur onto the thread. If necessary use fingernail varnish for this purpose. Wind back up to thorax. Dub chopped opossum fur over thorax. Tie in peacock herl over the thorax and finish off head with black head cement. The fibres should be left in a fairly rough state, but a little trimming to reduce bulk of fur may be necessary.

This nymph has become one of my favourites for back country or early season/heavy water use. Its debut was opening day on the Motueka, a number of seasons ago. The river was high and quite discoloured after some days of rain, so much so that I commenced fishing for the season with threadline gear. After hooking and losing three fish I decided that a change was necessary. As the day brightened I noticed that the margins were clearing somewhat so I plodded back to the car and rigged up my fly rod and tied on the untested M.M.

I stalked quietly along a bouldery run interspersed with quiet pocket water. As the mid-stream current was running full tilt I reasoned that the fish would by lying close in. Sure enough I had gone barely a dozen metres when the beautiful sight of a feeding fish appeared in a tiny pocket. I watched for a few moments as the trout swung from side to side taking nymphs.

A couple of false casts to the side and with a little prayer the tyro nymph was sent on its way. Too short. The nymph plopped into the water right on the fish's tail. With a sigh of relief I realised that it had not been alarmed. Once more into the breach, dear friends. This time there was no mistake. Almost imperceptibly the M.M. plopped into the water just a metre above and 15 cm to the right of the brown. A deliberate turn to the right and a slight rise in the water left no doubt that the ruse had worked. A steady lift of the rod was all that was needed to set the hook. The season was off to a great start and the M.M. had begun its career. In the next hour and a half, five more trout came to the net — all taken on the same nymph.

Just days later I had the good fortune to fish in my personal paradise — a back country river which shall remain unnamed. Suffice it to say that the M.M. passed with flying colours. On one day I landed close to a dozen fine trout averaging around 2.5 kg. Halcyon days indeed. All but three of these fish were taken on the M.M., good enough to convince me that it is a pattern worth persevering with.

"A dozen other patterns would have worked just as well," I hear you mutter. Perhaps so. Perhaps so. I still believe I've developed a successful nymph all the same.

The Problem Of Over-fishing

Most of the points raised here will be covered in more detail in the chapter on conservation. However, the writers feel so strongly about this issue that some of the points are worth raising more than once.

I was once naive enough to believe that the trout fishing in many back country rivers was almost limitless. Some of my first trips were into the middle section of the now well-known Karamea river. This area has substantial earthquake lakes formed by the damming of the river in the 1929 Murchison earthquake. It is a strange, damp, often humid, almost eerie environment. But as well as harbouring vast numbers of huge eels, these lakes on the river held prodigious quantities of brown trout. They were easy to catch. I recall one day when I cast my black and gold Toby ten times and hooked nine fish. I didn't land them all but a significant number were landed, the hooks pulled out and the trout released. Each day we dined royally on some of the trout we caught.

The fishing is still by most standards good in these lakes, but the trout are in no way the suckers they once were. In fact, they can become very cagey and difficult to fool, especially with spinning gear. The area is on a popular tramping route, and annually hundreds of people now pass by these lakes to penetrate even further into the rapidly diminishing wilderness. Coupled with helicopters bringing in many parties, the whole area is getting something of a thrashing. The big question is just how long the pressure can be sustained, especially on the tributary streams, some of which contain small numbers of fish.

Regrettably, I see an inevitable need for stringent regulations to prevent the demise of the goose which lays the golden eggs. Back country fishing is one of this country's greatest assets. We must see that it remains so.

7

Threadlining

A typical successful threadlining expedition may be a little like the one enjoyed by Les and myself one Labour Weekend a few years ago. Labour weekend has always been popular with the writers, as the trout invariably seem to take well. Perhaps the combination of longer days and slightly warmer water temperatures, combined with the relative lack of fishing pressure, make the fish less wary. However, on this occasion prospects looked rather grim. A warm, moist northerly had been dumping inches of rain over the preceding days causing a major fresh in most Nelson rivers. In fact, by the Friday evening of the holiday the Motueka River was higher than I had ever seen it before. Farm land was inundated and logs, trees and even fences tumbled down in the spate. We retired in a dismal frame of mind that night, quite convinced that fishing would be impossible for the entire week-end.

Saturday dawned bright and clear. The pristine, washed appearance of the countryside combined with joyful birdsong elevated our spirits considerably. A journey of 20 metres to the front gate confirmed that the river was still in a state of flood although already showing signs of dropping. A leisurely, relaxed breakfast followed and the conversation became at least a little more animated than on the previous evening. By 10 a.m. we could tolerate sitting around no longer and determined to drive a few kilometres to the Wangapeka River in the vain hope that it might be a little lower than the Motueka. Surprisingly, despite the fact that it drained much more rain-prone country, the Wangapeka was actually a more promising sight. As it drained largely forested land it was carrying much less silt. Nonetheless, it was bank to bank, but dropping quickly judging by the high water mark. We decided that we might as well at least go through the motions of trying to catch a trout. The brilliant sunshine and golden Kowhais helped to raise our spirits.

Les cast a black and gold Toby into the slack water behind a group of large granite outcroppings. These rocks deflected the enormous power of the river and created a natural quiet spot. No sooner had the line straightened up as it swung out of the edge of the current into the calm water, than a solid, slashing strike nearly wrenched the rod into the river. A golden-sided brown trout of around 2 kg leapt clear of the river and crashed sideways back into the murky water, free of the terrible trebles. Serious fishing commenced immediately, with every tiny pocket and eye probed by the deadly Toby. We soon discovered more fish. Many were lost, but within a couple of hours we both had heavy bags.

The tactics were simple: find quiet or clearing water. Fish were to be found in six main parts of the river; (a) pockets amongst and behind large rocks, (b) eyes of pools, (c) where clearer sidestreams entered the main stream, (d) backwaters, (e) lee of bank extensions, (f) towards the tail. With the water being so discoloured, we found the best approach to be a downstream one. This involved casting the heavy metal lure well out into the main current and letting it swing around until it was being retrieved upstream, often just a few metres from the bank, or just away from the main current if fishing eyes of pools or runs.

One point which cannot be over-stressed is that when fishing dirty water, speed of the retrieve is critical to success. It is necessary to retrieve as slowly as possible without actually becoming hooked up on the bottom. If the angler is applying full concentration it is usually possible to dislodge the lure from the bottom with a quick lift and flick of the rod top. There is no doubt in my mind that the slower the retrieve the greater the number of strikes, especially in very discoloured water.

The weekend turned into a resounding success despite the inauspicious beginning, indicating that trout can be caught even in conditions usually considered impossible. Back country streams in particular are subject to a rapid rise and fall. Consequently, the trout become attuned to this and can survive even the most terrible of floods probably by seeking out quiet water. As rivers clear, though, so the trout regain their natural wariness. Nelson's Wangapeka is a prime example. It is a heavily fished river throughout its length. As a result, even when the water is quite discoloured, spinning lures fished downstream in the conventional manner are rarely successful except when fishing at change of light in the morning and evening. In lightly discoloured water the tactics necessary for even modest success are strikingly different from those successful when the water is really murky. This is when active stalking, even spotting individual fish, will produce results. The angler needs to don polaroids and a wide-brimmed hat and become a hunter, as a careful approach becomes essential.

I know anglers who have amazing success stalking fish in this manner, even in the lowest water of mid-summer. The method is as sporting as any when the gear and the techniques used are taken into account.

Occasionally, one still runs into a purist fly fisherman, the type who loudly condemns anyone who would even deign to own a spinning outfit. I even know of a chap who describes himself as a 'dry fly' angler. Indeed, he refuses to budge from his conviction that the use of anything but surface flies is unsporting, and that even those who use weighted nymphs are just a little suspect. As for threadlining — well, that is talking heresy altogether.

I have had some potentially good days spoiled by threadliners fishing downstream with 12 g metal lures in the height of mid-summer. I've also had my fishing spoiled by canoeists and rafters, not to mention the fly fisherman who overtakes you and wades through all the likely runs in the next kilometre or so.

Most 'chuck and chance' threadliners have the good sense to give up after the first month or so as they simply don't catch the fish in the same numbers as in the early part of the season. Some have the sense to adapt their methods by using more appropriate equipment and techniques, or 'retire', for the season convinced that the river has been 'fished out', an assumption that is rarely correct, especially when fishing for brown trout.

Illust. 62
Threadliner versus fly
fisher.

109

It is my contention that intelligent use of threadline gear should be the stand-by of everyone who fishes seriously for trout. I have experienced many occasions when the use of my light spinning rod has put fish in the bag when conventional fly fishing techniques would have been well-nigh impossible.

I recall one occasion when the true worth of the spinning rod and reel really saved the day for me. On reaching our chosen river, my companion for the day, Smithy, and I were quite disappointed to find that the water was discoloured even though there had been little rain. Obviously the distant thunder of the previous evening had produced quite a cloudburst in the valley headwaters. Luckily, I had, as an afterthought, tossed my spinning gear into the boot of the car. Although the river appeared to be clearing somewhat, I elected to spin. Smithy was not particularly confident, but set up his fly rod and tied on a heavily weighted nymph. My spinning gear was set up with a Toby.

My companion walked downstream intending to fish the pockets and runs back up to the car. I walked up a little to the road bridge spanning the river and followed a forest road downstream. Thirty or forty minutes later we were opposite one another, on each side of the river about 2 km below the car. Almost immediately I regretted not choosing my fly rod, as the river was clearing rapidly — so often the case after a localised storm. It was now possible to see into the pockets and eyes, and although the water was still quite murky, fish could be seen lying close into the bank. My too hasty decision to set up the spinning gear was confirmed moments later when I was subjected to a whoop of joy and the sight of a heavily bent rod on the other side of the river. I began fishing, spinning all the likely water. For thirty minutes or so I'd had not a touch, though the odd dark shape had followed the lure from the depths without touching it, always a sure sign that the water is too clear for large spinning lures. Far upstream, my mate was into his third fish. As I rounded a slight bend I came to a classic 'eye' at the top of a long boulder-studded run.

Predictably, right on the edge of the fast main current water and the slack water was an absolute sitter for a nymph. The trout was feeding as if there were no tomorrows, weaving up to a metre each side as it intercepted nymphs dislodged by the recent fresh. If ever I'd regretted leaving my fly rod in the car this was the time. I tried one cast with my spinning lure. The Toby was summarily ignored without a break in the feeding pattern.

Back to the drawing board. Pondering my situation I sat with back against a flood-smoothed beech log. Almost instantly I recalled something I'd read years earlier and began searching feverishly through my bag. I soon discovered a bubble and container of split shot, but alas, I'd left my fly box back at the car. Frantically, I searched every dusty plastic container and finally discovered a dark-bodied, very battered looking wet fly in about size 10. I pulled the wings off and examined critically a presentable nymph. The bubble was tied to the line and 50 or 60 cm of light nylon added to form a trace with the fly on the end. A couple of exploratory casts showed that the whole outfit was a bit light, so I added water to the plastic bubble and found that it cast well. Now to test the set-up. A careful overhead cast placed the bubble in the white water at the head of the run.

Hardly daring to breathe I watched the bubble pass over the still feeding trout — no response. Again and again I tried until the reason for the lack of interest suddenly hit home. The 'nymph' was floating just under the surface and the fish simply wasn't seeing it. Hastily I pinched a piece of shot 15 cm above the fly. This time there was no mistaking the deliberate move of the fish and the flash of white as the nymph was engulfed. I waited until the fish straightened again, and struck hard to take up the slack and set the hook. The water exploded as the startled trout felt the hook. Ten minutes later this happy angler eased a fine 2 kg hen onto a sandy shore at the tail of the run.

Illust. 63
Nymph, bubble and
threadline.

GRANTWINTER

The method continued to work that day and has provided many a fine fish on subsequent occasions. A bubble and nymph actually has some advantages over traditional fly gear. It is ideal on small, overgrown streams where a backcast is impossible. For me though, the method is most useful in two situations; (a) in eyes of pools where a spotted fish is feeding actively, (b) in relatively shallow water (30-50 cm) over a stony bottom, particularly in low water conditions.

In the former situation the method can be deadly, providing the nymph is presented at the correct depth and the cast is made as directly upstream as possible. With experience, it is possible to attain as near a drag-free drift as one is likely to achieve using any method, by maintaining the merest hint of contact with the bubble. Usually, the first sign that a fish has taken the nymph is a distinct dip of the bubble. It is imperative that the fisherman keep his eyes firmly fixed on the bubble — not easy to do in broken water on a bright day.

When fishing riffly runs in the height of midsummer, the method comes into its own. It is the only method I know which enables a nymph to be fished virtually drag free over a long distance. It enables the angler to cover much more water than with normal fly gear and with considerably more delicacy. I've introduced complete novices to this method with startling success.

A couple of hot, dry summers ago I made a novice angler very happy with this method. My brother, resident in the North Island, was just getting into trout fishing and had had a modest degree of success with traditional spinning lures in some of the Hawkes Bay rivers. To date, though, his best fish was only one of around a kilogram. I was determined that he was going to catch a trout to be proud of before he left Nelson. The only snag was that the rivers were running typically low in the middle of January and normal 7 g lures were quite out of the question. I decided to try bubble and fly again.

On the first evening we went to a long, riffly run which just screamed trout. The well-oxygenated, boulder-studded run was perfect. I'd been catching a few fish in the evening using Green Beetle dry flies, so I tied on a size 10 beetle imitation and left Terry happily casting diagonally upstream, concentrating with all his might on the plastic bubble bobbing along in the increasing gloom, while I cast nymphs blind along the bouldery edge.

Suddenly I heard a mighty splash and a shout of delight simultaneously as a brown trout of prodigious proportions crashed onto the surface. What a sight for sore eyes. Unfortunately, delight soon turned to despondency as seconds later the rod straightened and the nylon went slack. The fish had broken off, and the reason soon became obvious when I checked the tension of the reel. In our haste to commence fishing we had both overlooked the need to adjust the drag setting — an expensive oversight, and one I am frequently reminded of by my brother who now insists that the fish was one of at least 3 kg.

We redeemed ourselves, though, the following day, fishing on a similar stretch of water some kilometres upstream. Again, I was nymphing along the edge and Terry was working the faster water in the middle of the stream. Twice I saw the bubble stop and dip in the current, and twice brother was too slow as each came off with a flurry. He was simply not striking quickly enough to set the hare and copper nymph. On the third occasion the bubble stopped I yelled 'strike!' This time the reaction was quick enough and the fight was on. After a spirited battle a fine 2 kg jack flopped on its side in the sandy shallows and was unceremoniously helped out of the water by a well-aimed boot. My pupil was ecstatic, and insisted on calling it a day there and then so that we could celebrate the event.

Despite the success obtainable by this method, probably the most fascinating method, requiring much more skill, is to stalk individual fish, particularly in pocket water where a very close approach is necessary, using nothing more than a few pieces of split shot on the line and a nymph on the end. Obviously, one cannot hope to cast 3-4 kg breaking strain line like this. The angler is forced into the 1-2 kg class lines, and particularly those with a very low diameter to breaking strain ratio. This is fishing at its best — meticulous stalking techniques, short, accurate casts and perfect timing of the strike. Whoever said threadlining isn't sporting?

One disadvantage of the method is that very light nylon is not conducive to rapid landing of fish and means that many fish may be too exhausted to survive if released. The angler will need to consider carefully whether or not the object is killing or releasing fish.

Lures

Large, heavy lures and line of 3-4 kg breaking strain are fine early season or whenever rivers are running high and discoloured. I'll fish confidently downstream with a 7 g black and gold Toby at times, and firmly believe that this is the most appropriate method for putting fish on the bank in heavy, dirty water. However, the stalking threadliner, especially the type who chooses to fish on the hot summer days, has to adapt to changing circumstances.

I always carry a range of tiny, Veltic and Mepps spinners with the flashing, revolving blade. These are often deadly in riffly water and when whisked across the nose of trout obviously nymphing in a run, pocket or eye of a pool. Strangely, trout will often devour such strange offerings when they are discriminating enough to refuse a well presented size 14 nymph. Whether the flashing of the lure is seen as food or simply stirs feelings of aggression I know not, but work these lures certainly do — at least for a significant part of the time. Few experiences can rival that of observing a large, angry brown chasing and slashing viciously at a clearly visible spinning lure. Sometimes, a trout will move a considerable distance to intercept such an offering.

Some years ago Les and I were carefully negotiating a bluff above a deep, clear pool. As we moved cautiously from handhold to handhold we noticed that the pool contained five or six big browns. They

Photo 47
Fishing upstream in clear
water.

were largely of academic interest owing to our precarious position. However, we soon reached a place where we could sit down amongst the riverbank foliage some five metres above water level. The trout were feeding quite actively in the depths of the pool with the odd one rising to near the surface, apparently to take a rising nymph or some sunken terrestrial.

"Have a go," said Les, indicating the spinning rod I was carrying, already set up with a small Mepps. Rather dubiously I decided it was worth a try so I cast right across the pool and allowed the lure to sink to the bottom. Then I slowly began the retrieve. The clarity of the water was such that even a number of metres beneath the surface the lure was clearly visible. After a couple of turns of the handle I noticed that one of the fish had spotted the lure and was tailing it.

"Wind faster," urged Les, and as I sped up, the trout unhesitatingly snatched the lure and was hooked firmly in the corner of the jaw. Eventually, I succeeded in quietening the fish down somewhat after it raced around the pool a few times shaking its head like a dog with a rat. At some risk of a ducking, Les managed to clamber down to the water's edge and release the trout which we estimated at close to 3 kg. The episode was quite a talking point on the long trudge back to the hut.

The Americans are great innovators in the world of trout fishing, and have been responsible for debunking many myths associated with angling generally. Amongst many recent gear innovations is the use of soft rubber worm type lures. The Mr Twister range is extensive, and while many of the lures are better for sea fishing, some are ideally suited to ultra-light spinning for trout.

I recently hooked and lost a very large trout, which I estimated at 4 kg plus, on a Mr Twister natural colour worm. The river was well above normal so I was probing pockets behind large boulders with a Toby lure. I'd hooked a few fish which had unfortunately come unstuck, so I was further galled when a big fish followed the lure right to my feet without taking. Past experience has indicated that persevering with the same lure is usually pointless in this situation, so I changed to a Mr Twister worm and pinched three pieces of shot at intervals on the rather heavy line, above the lure. I pitched the worm into the quite murky pocket and allowed it to drift freely in the current.

Before long the line stopped moving, and in the belief that it was stuck on the bottom I flicked the rod tip up. As I did so I felt a solid weight which moved rapidly towards the turbulent mid-river current. Suddenly, the obviously angry fish leapt from the water and literally skidded madly across the surface. I gasped at the sheer size of the fish and watched dumbfounded as line tore off the spool. Regaining my senses I lifted the rod tip and determined to try to exert some control. Again it came to the surface and skidded across it. I regained some line as it came back into quieter water but then it panicked and broached sideways on to the current and allowed itself to be carried along. With no space to manoeuvre in, I tightened up on the fish in a last, vain attempt to turn it, and crashed through some bankside scrub before being hopelessly blocked by a large willow leaning out over the river. Had the river been a little lower I'd have gone in clothes and all, but discretion dictated that I stay on the bank. The trout never stopped and the 3.8 kg line snapped like cotton, leaving a shaking and somewhat crestfallen angler in its wake. The worst part is the polite but patronising attitude of people when recounting the incident to them. Why is it always the biggest ones that get away?

Mr Twister lures of the kind mentioned are extremely versatile and can be used somewhat like a large nymph in low water conditions.

Trout certainly love the ones I've tried. As yet I haven't plucked up enough courage to use the very brightly coloured ones in a range of fluorescent shades. I'm sure that at times they are quite irresistible. After all, one needs only to look at the Glo Bug revolution at Taupo and marvel at the wierd and wonderful things catching fish there.

No matter what kind of lure is being used I am firmly of the opinion that single hooks work better than trebles. I'm sure that a single hook penetrates better and holds more effectively than trebles, which are too often thrown at the moment of the strike. Trebles cause terrible mutilation, and should not be used if fish are to be released.

Rods And Reels

The stalking threadliner needs to choose a rod every bit as carefully as the fly fisherman. To my mind a rod suitable for ultra-light spinning should be at least 2 m in length, be supple enough to cast lures down to 3 g, a reasonable distance without excessive effort, and yet have enough backbone to handle a hard fighting fish. My personal favourite is a Trent hollow glass rod. Unfortunately, it is not quite as good as it once was as about 14 cm of the tip was broken off by a careless client. Nonetheless, I find it works well in most situations, especially when the reel is loaded with soft monofilament of around 1.5 kg breaking strain.

Over the years I've used a lot of reels, but none has survived the test of time as well as my Mitchell Garcia 300A. I'm rough on gear and don't give it the loving care it deserves, yet this reel, not as flashy looking as many models around these days, has given many hundreds of hours of service without maintenance apart from slight adjustments to the bail arm from time to time.

A spare spool is very useful so that two line weights can be used as required. Backing in the form of heavier line is sensible, otherwise it may take hundreds of metres of nylon to fill the spool. Be sure to trim the knot joining the line carefully, though, as the cut-off ends can inhibit the free flow of line off the spool.

All too often I see people, especially youngsters, trying to cast lures with only half a spool of line. Spools must be filled almost to the very edge of the lip to obtain optimum casting efficiency.

Opinions vary as to the best knot to use when tying on lures or swivels. I prefer the locked half blood knot with only three or four turns. I always wet the knot with saliva before drawing it taut. One caution — it is easy to tighten this knot too far causing it to cut through.

Likely Threadlining Lies

This aspect has been thoroughly covered in earlier chapters of *Stalking Trout*. Nonetheless, some significant differences are worth noting, especially as threadlining often takes place when the river is in higher than normal flow. Obviously eyes of pools and runs are likely to hold feeding fish most of the time, no matter what the level of the river and are the areas to concentrate on.

Photo 48
Threadlining to eye of
pool.

When a river is flooded, the trout's primary concerns are to find shelter and sanctuary and to obtain enough food to sustain itself. The thinking angler concentrates on areas likely to provide the first-mentioned, and nothing provides this better than a friendly boulder, deep hole, bank extension or backwater.

Not long ago I had firsthand experience of trout reaction to a significant rise in river level. This incident occurred in a back country river where trout have to be alert to these sudden and dramatic changes.

Early in the day I had carefully fished up through a delightful run and had spotted only one fish. Around midday, the rain which had been threatening struck with a vengeance. At 4 p.m. it eased, so I left the shelter of the hut and, as much to stretch the legs as anything else, I walked upstream 15 minutes to the same stretch. The river had risen, but only slightly, and had the slightest touch of colour in it. As I watched, the level rose quite markedly. As if according to some pre-arranged cue, trout began to appear in the run. In the space of 30 minutes I hooked four fish and landed one. Interestingly, the fish were

Photo 49
Threadlining in pocket
water.

all lying in the quiet pockets rapidly forming among large boulders. In retrospect, I realised that the fish had chosen a spot which would have provided the sanctuary in even a major flood. Therefore, for me, pocket water with the buffer it offers is a prime area through which to fish a lure. Both Les Hill and myself have observed fish moving to the surface of a pool or run as a river rises. We once watched a number of large fish do this and feed actively right on the surface before simply disappearing. We surmise that these are fish on the move, using the rising river level to migrate to safe havens.

Some rivers have numerous backwaters which in normal or low flow don't have enough water in them to hold fish. These same places can become the 'hotspots' on the river as the flood waters rise. I have one such favourite place on the Motueka River which produces time after time. Parts of this particular backwater are so shallow that the fish lie with fins almost out of the water. The action is usually fast and furious as the trout, often around 2 kg, pounce avidly on the lures worked tantalisingly past their noses. Low water threadline lies are likely to be popular with the local trout population for other reasons. One is the need for oxygenated water, and unless water temperatures are excessively high, for food also.

One summer I found that river levels dropped alarmingly in the latter part of January and the fishing became very hard during the day. I wasn't seeing anything like the numbers of feeding fish that I had only weeks earlier, so I decided to experiment with ultra-light spinning lures in the fastest water I could find (except where it actually went over a fall). The results were most encouraging. Sometimes I could barely discern a fish in the white water, at other times I cast up into the rapids anyway, and was often surprised by the ferocity of the strike as the fish hit the little Veltics. I lost a lot of fish on the strike or soon after, but caught enough to make the method worth persevering with.

Photo 50
Threadlining in tail of pool.

Illust. 64
A stalking threadliner.

The critics of threadlining as a method are, I suspect, often those who have done very little of it. I've been fortunate to have fished with some very talented spin fishermen, and if a little of that expertise has rubbed off, I am very grateful. Some of the most skilful, delicate angling I have ever seen has been with a 2 m spinning rod and ultra-light line and lures. The stalking spin fisherman who really thinks about his fishing has every right to be regarded as a legitimate angler in his own right. If this chapter has provided just a few ideas for basically 'chuck and chance' threadliners, then it will have achieved its purpose.

8

Favourite Stalking Places

The Motueka: A River For All Tastes

The Motueka.

Spring is a magic time for me, and spring to this angler starts on October 1st, the opening of the trout fishing season. Sure, the signs are apparent much sooner, but September is a long, dismal month as it drags itself tardily along. No matter what the weather though, October 1st is the most glorious day of the year, as good as many Christmases rolled into one, imaginary battles on the river looming uppermost. I feel genuine pity for those who don't look forward to an opening day of some kind.

For some seven years I lived with a view of the upper Motueka River from my front gate. The house was situated on an elevated ancient river terrace just seven long minutes walk from the tail of a favoured run. At a glance I could assess the state of the river. Indeed, after nights of heavy rain the roar of the river was enough to tell of its swollen state.

Such proximity to a river as delightful as the Motueka spoils one. Now, living an hour away, I wonder why I didn't fish more frequently when I lived so close. It is possible to develop an intimacy, and even

Fiordland stream.

121

possessiveness about such a gift. Certainly, I came to know its quirks well. Throughout the season I could pinpoint with a fair degree of accuracy just where the fishing was likely to be 'on'. This intimate knowledge has since proved to be a great advantage.

I fished all legal methods in my time at Tapawera and enjoyed success with them all. The Motueka River for most of its length, and especially below its confluence with major tributaries, the Wangapeka and Baton, is a wide, stately river flowing gracefully between well-defined, willow-lined banks. There is room aplenty for many anglers whether they be threadliners, live baiters, upstream fly fishermen or, particularly in the middle and lower reaches, wet fly fishermen. These latter may account for the greatest number of trout throughout the season. They tend to fish almost exclusively in the long, balmy summer evenings and rarely move from certain favoured places — usually long, sparkling runs full of trout averaging around one kilogram. I prefer the less crowded upper sections of the river around the busy forestry settlement of Tapawera. Even at the height of the holiday season I rarely see another fisherman on 'my' patch.

My most memorable experience came one typically sunny February day when picnicking with family and friends. I wasn't really fishing seriously at all but decided to have a short stroll up river a little after lunch. After a few minutes I came to a deep, clear pool where the river turned a prominent bend. There were always fish in this spot, but normally they lay right on the bottom three or four metres down where they sought respite from the strong current nearer the surface.

As usual, through 'windows' which appeared in the surface turbulence I spied three large shadowy shapes moving gently from side to side, accepting morsels off the bottom. Naturally I tried a few half-hearted casts — first with a large dry fly which I hoped would entice one of the big fellows upwards. No such luck. Mechanically I changed to my heaviest nymph — a well weighted stone-fly imitation. This was cast well upstream in the vain hope that it would get somewhere near the speckled beauties. On the third and fourth cast I fancied I saw one of the trout rise from the bottom some distance.

Dispensing with caution I threw a long line right up into the rapid above the pool. As the nymph passed over the trout I noticed the same fish as before lift markedly in the water in an attempt to intercept the nymph. Too late, but not to be outdone the large shape turned 180° and followed the fly as it drifted towards the tail of the pool. I was convinced it would be alarmed by the sight of me stripping in the line frantically, but still it continued its pursuit until at a point some two or three metres below me I clearly observed large jaws clamping down on the fly.

Seconds seemed like hours as I waited until the fish moved away from me before striking. The fight which followed was an anti-climax. With the fish held hard on a short line it wasn't long before it lay gasping on the sandy bank. I gasped in turn as its full depth became apparent. It was a beauty — a short, thick jack in prime condition — all 3.3 kg of it. It was my best fish from the river over a ten year period and of a size which many seasoned Motueka River anglers only dream of catching.

Whether one chooses to fish for whitebait-gorged sea runs at the mouth or stalk amazingly difficult one and two kilogram fish upstream in the height of summer, the Motueka is a river for all tastes.

Photo 53
Fiordland stream.

A Fiordland Stream

It's not as good as it once was. Recent floods destroyed it — choked the bed with fine gravel — almost sand. Yet I'm reluctant to reveal its name. It may recover. I'll keep watching.

Nestled in Fiordland it's not a spectacular place. Log jams hinder the flow and hide the trout. The current is never swift and the slightly eely water rarely clears. The stream runs confined by ferny, well-wooded banks. From the air it's almost invisible. It meanders endlessly.

There are few trout and I've never seen one more than 2kg. Maybe that's why no one ever fishes there, few to my knowledge anyway. These are the attractions — solitude, uniqueness, challenge. The first time I went there I left my rod at home. I was deer stalking one May and wasn't aware the fishing season remained open. For a week I stalked the river's banks and surrounds. For a week I watched trout feeding freely in the midday sun. I cannot deny I was tempted to 'pot' one as it broke the surface, but resolved to wait for November.

That first fishing trip (there have been several since) was the best. It had the mystery of discovery. Visiting new places is always like that. I was exhausted at the end of that day, physically exhausted, as was my companion, Eden Shields. Eden had been there in May too. He hadn't known about the extended season either; we had planned to return together, and here we were, a dream fulfilled.

One of the satisfying things about the stream was that it had few patterns. It meandered in an ill defined direction with its tangled mass of logs. With little fast water the trout had no need to seek refuge from energy-sapping flow — only from anglers. A stalking angler needed no knowledge of reading water — seeking eyes, lee sides and tails — they didn't exist. There were no expected places, the fish were where you found them.

How many experiences grow in reminiscence? Most I suspect. Re-telling and re-dreaming days past tends to cloud and enshroud un-pleasantries. Excitement and good times mushroom to become favour-ed memories. Rare are the moments which at the time match retro-spective experience, yet our first day on this hallowed stream was one of those rare times.

One ripply reach epitomized our day. I can clearly remember the two of us standing amid shoulder-high scrub laughing heartily, uncon-trollably. Five minutes earlier we had been full of concentration. Two trout, unaware we watched, fed eagerly within casting distance up-stream from a mass of tangled logs, so entangled they spanned and enveloped the stream. In doing so they provided a firm casting plat-form, yet at the same time offered beneath a refuge for startled fish.

Eden cast first. Keeping his backcast high to avoid upright branches, he lengthened his line then finally shot it forward and to the side of the lower trout. The response was instant — a drift leftwards, a slight rise then the fly disappeared. An initial panic-stricken thrash preceded a mad dash beneath our feet deep into the logs. Cunning? Experienced? Instinct more likely. Trout one, anglers nil!

The second fish fed quietly, oblivious to proceedings. My turn. Description is unnecessary. My act mirrored Eden's and the fish's response was the same as the first. I was left holding a lifeless rod and severed line. Trout two, anglers nil! One of the specialities of the stream.

Concealing ourselves in scrub close to the water we journeyed on. Around another curve revealed more undermined banks and fallen trees dipping midstream, a productive part of the river. Matching the brackish tinge of the water a dark flanked brown ranged wide for all offerings. With the previous excitement still abating and the knowl-edge of what confronted us we could not suppress our angler's joy. There was nothing funny happening, yet we started laughing — not public relations laughter — real laughter.

As I said, there were not many fish in the stream, but those we saw were hungry. We hooked most. The majority were swallowed by logs and lost. I wouldn't want it any other way because that's what makes the place what it is.

Such uniqueness cannot adequately be described to others. The only way to share it is to go there. I hope it means soon.

The Ohape

One is never alone on the Ohape — an unheralded stream near Temuka. Flowing through pasture and cropland this spring-fed creek has inhabitants and visitors throughout its length. There are the hopeful anglers of course, crusing a narrow path through tall grasses, but more in harmony are the inquisitive cows who occasionally wallow, the horses, the sheep, the skylarks and the insects. The insects are the pulse

*Photo 54
The Ohape.*

125

of the stream, ever moving, ever present. A moment's hesitation, observation, reveals their variety and abundance. Mayflies drift and hatch all day. Caddis abound, while dragonflies perform their capricious dance in mid-flight. One hovered overhead as I crouched, wondering how I could possibly get a fly to a 40 cm trout which drifted in search of surface life. The stream was no more than three metres wide with willows hanging precariously low. A back handed side cast was the only possibility — if I could avoid the grasses behind. A 1.5 m leader aided the task of accuracy, but also demanded it.

I swung the rod up over my left shoulder, keeping the line short, then pushed forward and rightwards with my thumb. False casts would only add possibilities of being hooked in grass or willow. The tiny Dad's Favourite sped forward and settled short and too far to the right. For those of us who have difficulty in open spaces and with the accuracy of overhead casting, placing a side cast calls for guess work and correction, not to mention a short prayer. Aim to the left was the answer from above. The second flick landed closer. Further to the left was the next command. My helper knew, third time lucky — the fly drifted close to the fish's nose. A trout's control and command in the water is sublime. A subtle inclination of the fins — the interception precise. I watched the floating nylon tightening before striking. Success! Unless there are snags nearby there is little a fighting fish can do except dart about, broach, or duck under weeds and bank. However, the net soon eased the fish bankwards, the hook was extracted easily and the fish regained its freedom.

Unknown to me at the time, an angling lesson had just begun. Two days later I returned to the same stretch of river, and there, guarding the same position, was the 40 cm trout caught and released previously. There are not too many 40 cm fish in the Ohape. Another size 18 Dad's Favourite soon adorned the end of a 1.5 m leader and the unique hazards of side casting amid a jungle tackled.

With assistance and advice from the voice beyond, my casting neared its mark. Finally the tiny fly floated where it should. The trout acknowledged the fly and lifted its head, nosed the surface but declined the offer. Undisturbed, it continued to feed. The fly pattern was not acknowledged on further offering so a change was made — a Twilight Beauty. With contemptuous confidence the first good drift was taken and once more we engaged in a furious battle. Once more the fish was netted and dispatched to the stream quickly.

My curiosity became aroused. Had the fish remembered the first pattern it had been caught on? Was it showing an ability to learn and remember? To test this was an irresistible challenge.

Anglers have little difficulty in finding time or excuses to go fishing. Having established mine I returned to the Ohape to tempt my fish once more. Dutifully it occupied the same niche and ranged about as before. Having had plenty of casting practice in this tight spot I required less advice. My Dad's Favourite, the first temptation, initiated a sidewards drift and cursory inspection — nothing more. Now the Twilight Beauty. The backcast before the final push — that's the one — that's the time I always snag behind. Knowing more precision and full extension are essential, maybe I dip the rod a little lower. No matter what, it had to be unhooked. Back in position I tried again, and again. Patience and perseverance are an integral part of angling. At last the fly settled upstream of the trout, then floated closer. The fish rose, turned and pursued, ever cautious, but was not persuaded.

Next a Red Tipped Governor — my old standby, my favourite — I couldn't see it failing. In a way it didn't. The first time it drifted close, the fish pivoted on its tail, broke the surface and sucked it down. We made brief contact, just for one mad dash then the fish was free again. We were both content. He was free and I had learned, or was almost convinced, that trout quickly become discerning.

There lies the magic of the Ohape. I respect the stream because of the lessons it has to teach. It is a refining ground. Casting must be exact and repertoire expansive. The trout are not large, but their powers of survival are considerable. Heavy feet, large flies, thick tippets, line shadow — the pitfalls of every angler — are treated with deserved disdain. Small the trout may be — an opening for condescension — but think this way and you will receive the ultimate lesson in failure.

The Dream River

Can you picture the most perfect trout stream of all — the one you dream about? I can, and the truth of the matter is that it does exist. I know such a place. Others know my favourite stream now and in reality it is probably visited more often than I would like. Thankfully, most of those who visit it treat it with the same respect as I do. In some six or eight visits I've killed but four trout, and on future trips, for it is a long walk there, I will kill none unless it be the fish of my dreams, in excess of 4.5 kg.

You have realised by now that my unnamed stream is something special. It will also have become apparent that it requires a special effort to get there. Few walkers will do it under two and a half days, and once they arrive may be disappointed as the lower reaches are not particularly inspiring and the access difficult, especially after rain. If the gorgy, slippery entrance puts some aspirants off, so be it. Few good things come easily in the world of angling nowadays.

Once the gauntlet has been run you will begin to see what I mean. Steep, rain-forest covered slopes relent just enough for access up the valley. Sparse goat and deer trails trace a logical route. In low water good safe crossings make the going easier. Dally not if the river is rising though, as being restricted to just one bank makes for miserable travelling to avoid bluffs and rotten windfalls.

On a fine day the river is the perfect 'stream of one's dreams'. Deep, mysterious green pools give promise of big trout, and big trout there are — not in abundance mind, but enough to keep one in a constant state of high excitement. It's definitely not for the faint-hearted, this place.

*Photo 52
Dream stream.*

Time after time, particularly in the more heavily-fished lower reaches, the fish will have the last laugh as they disdainfully refuse the most tempting products of the fly. Super-clear water and a built-in natural caution ensure that most of these piscatorial aristocrats stay right where they belong.

My biggest trout was caught in one such pool — caught and then released because it didn't quite make the magic 4.5 kg mark. The day was anything but perfect, it was dull and grey with steady, persistent rain which managed to seep down our necks despite the best of waterproof clothing. A rising river and very poor light also helped to dampen our spirits.

Smithy was sneaking ahead peering into every likely eye and run when he spied a fish feeding avidly in the run just above a deep pool. He offered to spot for me and by concealing himself behind a handy coprosma, he could see the trout quite clearly without being detected himself. I had no hope of seeing the fish from my position so my casting had to be according to my mate's instructions.

The first cast landed just behind the fish but the next was right on the spot. There was no mistaking the take as the fish bulged just under the surface to take the large nymph. I paused briefly then struck. Almost simultaneously the startled trout thrashed on the surface before making a mad, panicking run into the murky depths of the pool. For perhaps twenty minutes I placed all the strain I dared on the trout without appearing to make any headway. I'd estimated the fish at about 2.5 kg judging by the brief glimpse I'd had of it and I was puzzled by my inability to move it. Eventually, though, it came off the bottom and another ten minutes of short runs in the sandy tail of the pool followed.

My companions were thoroughly wet and starting to feel the cold, so they exhorted me to land the fish so that they could proceed upriver. At great risk of breaking either leader or rod I did so and dragged ashore a still very strong fish. I couldn't believe my eyes when the short, stocky brown rolled over on its side. A very hurried conversation ensued and the weight was estimated at close to 4 kg — a good fish but not good enough for mounting, so the nymph was removed with surgical forceps, a photo taken and the fish released. I landed three fish that day with an estimated average weight of over 3 kg — a red letter day indeed despite the weather.

Just above the series of pools the valley suddenly opens out onto a broad scrubby flat interspersed with tiny patches of well-grazed grass. Two or three goats are nearly always viewed at this point and provide a brief diversion before the serious business of fishing recommences.

If asked to describe the perfect run in a river, the two or three hundred metres which stretch up from this point must come fairly close. The true right bank is a delight, giving access to a wonderful series of pockets behind large boulders. There are always fish along this edge and they are usually a little more easily caught than those inhabiting the shady pools in the heavy bush below. Perhaps this is why they are a little smaller than average for the river. Trout of 2-3 kg occupy most of the pockets and lies along this stretch.

At the very top though comes the *piece de resistance*. A deep pool has formed where the river makes an almost right-angled turn. There are always trout in this place — often as many as five or six. As yet I've not landed one despite a number of brief encounters. Just above here is the trickiest ford of all, and if the river is even a little high, not to be attempted. A long, tiring scramble through 3 m high scrub to a safer crossing is the only alternative. From this point on the pools are less frequent and turbulent, and white water holding but few fish is encountered more often. The holding places, though few in number, nearly always contain fish — often a solitary, sizeable beast, and infinitely desirable to the stalking angler.

Of course, though I've had some great days in this most favoured of places, I've had some totally blank ones too, but equally enjoyable as I've delighted in the success of my companions. It is indeed a wonderful place — the stuff of which dreams are made.

9

Conservation

After an unusually long dry spell in Fiordland the Lyvia River had assumed an apparently placid and harmless facade as it ambled seaward. Its crystal waters glided around massive boulders and ducked under overhanging beech branches seeking the next pool. Standing on a bridge high above the water, I gazed upstream as fishermen invariably do, hoping to sight a feeding trout. A long curving pool invited considerable attention. Deep, boulder-strewn and log-infested, it was one of those infallible places. Yet no dimples appeared, no shapes hovered. I reflected on a conversation with an officer in the Acclimatisation Society who told me that surveys proved that pools seemingly barren to a passing angler often contained healthy numbers of fish. 'Perhaps' I thought. The gin-clear waters seemed to reveal all.

As I contemplated, I became aware of a movement near the tail of the pool. A tangle of logs extended from the bank on my right. A bow wave pushed upstream from it. 'A Blue Duck,' I mused. A pair with a chick had fed nearby the previous day. The wave stopped and the pool regained its former tranquility for a moment.

Then further upstream a head popped out of the water. The alert eyes and twitching whiskers of a young seal were revealed. The animal stopped then drifted effortlessly with the current, taking in all around. It was obviously watching beneath the surface too because it dived without warning and sped, apparently unhindered by the current, first to its right then to its left and disappeared under an overhanging rock shelf.

Shocked and spellbound I waited for the reappearance. I was shocked because this was a foreign sight to me in a river and I was loath to share my trout with a seal. Besides, a seal is a much better fisherman than I am! The head emerged again but only momentarily. The sleek and efficient shape darted back along the shelf and this time emerged victorious. A seemingly lifeless trout of about 1 kg hung from the seal's tightly gripping jaws.

Wild animals are not only more efficient than man in capturing their prey but also waste less time in devouring it. This was quickly revealed to me by the seal. Obviously unsatisfied with one trout the hunt soon recommenced. Unable to compete in that pool I pushed on upstream hoping to find some water without another fisherman.

During the next few days I returned to the lower pools of the Lyvia. Despite ideal spotting conditions I saw few trout. Further upstream the numbers increased. My conclusion was that the numbers in the pools near the estuary were depleted by one, maybe more, seals.

Like the seal there are many anglers who are very efficient at catching trout and equally unheeding of the need to consider conservation of numbers. They are quite content to refish an area until a lack of success drives them elsewhere, unconcerned that they have taken all the river will yield.

I feel strongly that unless anglers dispel their seal-like mentality and are prepared to show care both directly and politically for their sport then we will all have to accept an ever-diminishing quality in fishing.

The real future of angling lies in the hands of the politicians, the farmers, the foresters, industrialists, miners and power developers. But anglers do have a say. The foundation of that 'say' lies in the anglers' hearts — in their personal attitudes and practices.

Photo 60
The future of rivers and fishing lies in the hands of land users and politicians.

Releasing Trout

The most obvious conservation practice for an angler is that of killing only the fish that are wanted for food and releasing those caught thereafter.

Superficially, releasing trout appears a simple matter — land the fish, remove the hook then replace the fish in the water. But trout which are being returned are, to the angler, regaining their freedom for just one reason, and that is that they might survive, hopefully bigger and fatter, to provide future sport.

To me there is no point in releasing trout unless it is done with the greatest of care and with a reasonable assurance that survival will

Illust. 65
Releasing a fish.

result. I am sure that others releasing fish feel the same, yet my observation of release in practice leaves doubts about survival rates. I envisage five principles which should be considered for successful release;
1.   The use of the strongest practical nylon tippets to facilitate quick landing of fish.
2.   The use of a wide-mouthed net for quick removal of fish from the water.
3.   The use of barbless hooks for ease and speed of removal.
4.   The use of artery forceps (or similar) to remove hooks quickly and reduce handling of fish.
5.   Great care in handling fish while on the hook.

Use Of Strong Tippets

At one time it was considered sporting to fish with delicate nylon tippets. It added finesse to the sport by compelling an angler to take great care and time in landing a fish. Probably the most sporting act in fishing today is that of releasing a fish. Evidence and logic suggest that to play a fish for a long time, as is necessary on light tackle, diminishes the chances of a released fish surviving. It makes sense then to reduce the landing time. Stronger nylon is one way of facilitating this. I commonly use nylon tippets of 2.5, 3 and 3.5kg where conditions allow. In rough, back country streams, in tumbling waters, 5.5kg line is practical and apparently invisible. On lowland streams and calm clear backwaters, the trout have time to consider each morsel carefully. Line shyness is more of a problem and obviously lighter tackle is necessary. But again one can be practical. If a breeze riffles the water or recent rain has slightly coloured a stream then a stronger line is possible. If release is the intention of an angler then minimal playing time should be kept well in mind.

A thoughtful angler should also consider carefully the line he uses. Manufacturers state, on spools of nylon, the breaking strength and diameter of the line. One can only have faith that their claims are accurate. I consider line strength, diameter and colour before purchasing, but more importantly I consider the effect of a knot on the breaking strength. When a knot is tied in nylon the strength is invariably diminished. The magnitude of change varies with different brands of nylon. It also varies with the manner in which a knot is tied. A knot tightened very quickly weakens the line more than one tightened slowly. An hour passed one wet day testing a number of readily available nylons with variously tied knots would be profitable to all anglers.

Equipped with the best lines and making a thoughtful choice of line strength, an angler should be more effective at landing fish more quickly.

At this time another complication could be noted. Size 16 and 18 flies are not particularly compatible with 3.5 kg tippets. The force one can exert with such strong line would in time straighten the hook. Fortunately in the place where strong line is best used, larger, stronger flies are successful.

In his book '*The Trout and the Stream*' Charles Brooks points out three important ideas for a fisherman releasing trout. Brooks says, "For releasing fish with the least amount of trouble and with the most assurance that the released fish will live, you must have a net." He proceeds to add . . . "Ruttner, in '*Fundamentals of Limnology*', says that fish under exertion or stress accumulate lactic acid of up to 9 times the rate that humans do under like conditions. When the acid in the system reaches certain levels, it becomes toxic and the fish is doomed."

Thus, a fish played until 'belly up' may appear to recover and swim off when released. But the acid accumulation is there and about seven times out of ten, your fish will die sometime later, within a day or so.

Ted Trueblood may have had this in mind when he condemned the use of ultra light tackle as being poor sportsmanship, because he said, a fish played until belly-up on such tackle usually died soon after. This is surely testimony indeed for us to consider strong tippets if our intention is to release a fish.

Use of An Adequate Net

A few minutes walk upstream from the Karamea Bend hut, there is a long, deep pool. On the wide gravelly western bank access is unobstructed and casting easy. The eastern bank is sheer and about 20 metres high. Thus it provides an excellent vantage point for watching the cruising trout in the pool or viewing an angler in action in the arena below.

Net too small.

*Photo 57
An adequate net is
essential to aid quick
landing.*

My brother Ho and I made our way along the high bank early one morning, planning to explore the waters further upstream. On the way we hesitated and pushed through dense scrub to peer down into the pool beneath us. We were confronted by an elderly gentleman, up to his knees in water, casting long and accurately to a fish, presumably more visible to us than him. With such an excellent view of both angler and fish we paused to watch the action. Both trout and angler were oblivious to our presence. How long the angler had been trying to lure the fish to the surface is questionable but within three casts of our arrival the hook was set, rod bowed acutely and reel screaming. The clarity of the water and our overhead position granted us a marvellous view of the trout's acrobatics below the surface.

The angler took the first opportunity to back out of the pool to pick up his landing net which lay on the sand. The handle when unfolded appeared long enough but the triangular mouth seemed awfully small compared to the trout. Net in hand our entertainer soon eased back into the water. He pushed forward until the water lapped his rolled-up trousers. Maybe he went that deep to get closer to the fish but I suspect it was more in order to protect his bare legs from the ever-present, eager sandflies.

Gradually the fish was edged closer and closer to the waiting net. But each time the net was sighted another desperate run ensued. Time and time again the angler tried to position the net accurately so that the fish could be slid in either tail or head first. Time and time again the trout just evaded his attempts. In desperation the angler lifted the net with the trout on top but the fish did not buckle and fall in. Instead it leaped clear and thrashed back into the water. The line held. The fish was eventually netted but only when its strength was completely sapped and it floated on its side gently waving its fins and tail and heaving its gills.

An adequate net is essential

We were pleased to see it being released but doubted its chances of survival. The angler had to hold the fish upright in the water and rock it gently forward and back to pass oxygen through its gills. When the fish eventually moved off it was very sluggish and obviously sick.

The release of that fish could have been quicker if the angler had remembered three things. First, he should have equipped himself with a more adequate net. By more adequate I mean the mouth should have been large enough to allow a large fish to be slipped in easily without too much manoeuvring. Second, the angler could have stirred up the muddy bed to create a zone of discoloured water. In the discoloured water the net would have been partially hidden. Net shyness is often avoided in this way. Third, the shore on which the fish was caught was very gently sloping and composed of fine sand and mud. Had the angler backed up the bank leading the fish on a long line I'm sure he would have halved the landing time and not damaged the fish as it thrashed about. My experience has been that by keeping well back from a fish and easing it into shallows by walking backwards with a constant pressure, trout succumb surprising easily even when full of life. But get too close to the fish or try winding it in and there is often more reluctance to be 'beached'. I would only 'beach' a trout where the ground would not damage the fish's flanks.

Adequate net.

The wife of a fishing companion asked me just before Christmas what her husband would appreciate as a gift. Knowing he always used my landing net and did not possess one of his own, I suggested the same. To assist further I visited a number of Invercargill retailers to see what was available. What I saw implied that the overseas manufacturers have designed for smaller fish than the three kg ones I feel a net should adequately cope with in New Zealand. Unfortunately availability leads to sales, and what I see anglers armed with generally verifies this. I am reluctant to be too critical of other anglers' equipment because I know at times I am nothing short of a hypocrite. I am not saying that I carry a small-mouthed net, but I can remember times when I left my net behind altogether. One day on the Monowai River springs to mind immediately.

The Monowai River is unique. The flow is monitored by control gates. When the gates are open, as they were on this particular day, the stream is full, bank to bank. The banks are overgrown with regenerating native bush. A hydrological gauging station has been erected not far below the control gates.

Directly downstream of the station is one of my favourite reaches in the river, where tall flax bushes hang lazily over the evergliding waters, and where streamside of the flax the water is too deep to wade. Bankside is a swampy jungle, a veritable nightmare to a right handed angler. To stalk the edges an angler must hang precariously over the flax yet try to move the vegetation as little as possible. I've scared more fish there than I've ever fished to.

This time luck accompanied me. Leaving my rod behind I stooped cautiously forward and used two hands to part the long leaves gently. Nothing there. I moved again. Parting a new set of leaves I was thankful for a gentle upstream breeze which riffled the water and moved other bushes, rendering my movements more natural. The next change of position was more fruitful. Just ahead a flax bush dipped its leaf tips into the river. They waved continuously downstream then recovered their position as they bounced back up. Under the arch of the flax a good sized rainbow hugged the bank and occasionally sipped flies from the surface. To cast directly upstream of the fish would be impossible — the only hope was to lure it out. A large bushy Red Tipped Governor seemed appropriate.

For me, fishing blind rarely presents any problems. It is a mechanical, smooth, regular pattern, a rhythmical relaxing style, fitting to the serenity of a trout stream.

Yet, place a trout in front of me, particularly one feeding visibly, and I can find, invent, exaggerate a multitude of problems in moments. Wind knots appear, the fly hooks onto the rod, bushes behind grab my fly, the line slips from my left hand — you name it, it happens. All honest fishermen will know what I am trying to convey. Amid luxuriant flaxes the inevitable occurred. Why the fish did not see or hear me scrambling and stomping around unhooking my fly ahead and behind, I'll never know. It continued selecting flies.

Two anglers working together.

I didn't manage to float a fly down outside the flax as planned but one cast did leap over the leaves and the loose end allowed the fly to pass near the fish. It was willingly selected. An initial lunge of the startled trout tore the line clear of all obstacles and a lengthy battle began. Not until the fish was hooked did I consider the problems of landing which lay ahead. Without a net or any clear bank there was no easy solution. In fact the only possibility lay in tiring the fish sufficiently for me to grab it in my hands and lift it clear of the bushes

140

Photo 59
Two anglers can land a
fish quicker than one.

— not an easy task with a lively 2 kg rainbow. By the time I could lean out and winch the fish in by hand it was totally submissive, nearly lifeless. There was no choice, the fish could not be returned to the river with a fair chance of survival. It is criminal enough to torture a fish with a poorly designed net but inexcusable to have intentions of releasing a fish and yet have no net on hand.

Among other benefits, two anglers fishing together are much more efficient at netting and releasing trout than a lone fisherman. With two hands operating rod and line plus the advantage of freedom of movement about the bank the successful fisherman can manipulate his catch to the netter who with just one job, has greater mobility and capability.

Barbless Hooks

Sports writers all, from time to time, get caught by desire or request to list and rank favourites of one type or other. It may be a team of all-time greats, the best ground or course and so on. I pondered recently my favourite fishing places and the water type in particular. My anticipation is always high when approaching a new pool, and ripples hold a fascination of their own. The productivity of eyes rate them highly while backwaters test one's patience and guile. Yet, when I picture the 'best' it is almost invariably pocket water — long, straight, bouldery reaches, myriads of pools and little glides, endless holding places and countless problems. Their variety renders them extra special.

Special too, and equally different are the shallows of lakes. There is one I have visited many times, a tiny lake by any standards. Not so tiny that one can't cast across — but almost. On all sides the banks are high, made higher by tall poplars and willows. In the autumn their browns and golds blaze with colour and at all times they yield to the wind, maintaining a relative stillness on the waters. From the shallow margins reeds and bulrushes grow and furnish an abundance of insects.

In fifteen minutes one angler can stalk the entire shore. It is not a place many anglers go to. It's one of these havens one approaches hoping to find it deserted.

Last autumn I was drawn by the charm of the place once again. You can imagine my disappointment at hearing the voices of two anglers already absorbed in battle. They did not notice my approach so I stood some distance back and watched.

One angler spotted and pointed, issuing excited instructions while the other cast to an obviously cruising trout. The forward cast curled out quickly, expending all energy, then the line descended the final foot, sedately and softly. All became motionless for a moment. The hopeful angler was bent forward, head down, arms outstretched. His companion watched the fly intently. A wind-riffled surface obscured the lake but the buckle of rod and scream of reel revealed success. Contact with the fish lasted only a few seconds but long enough to extract whoops of joy and hearty laughter from the two ahead of me. Their disposition transformed the moment they saw me, rod in hand about to intrude. Mumbled greetings preceded a guarded conversation predominantly reporting the lack of fish and poor conditions. Another pond, a short walk away, sounded immeasurably superior.

When it became apparent that we would have to share the little lake the talk loosened to an exchange of advice. Having patiently received a good share I shifted to stalk the opposite shore. Restricted fishing space can have its benefits. I have noticed it slows an angler down, adding to his care. I knew that only two chances would appear in the next hour. All nonchalance was expelled, no short cuts considered.

Kneeling amid lofty rushes I glanced back and forth waiting for the movement I knew would appear. Five minutes is a long time, ten an eternity. Still no shape. Then the silence was broken by a tell-tale slurp. Approaching from my left the culprit glided nearer. "Wait until it's moving away," I warned myself. "I can't take a risk." Eventually 8 m separated us so I hastily stripped the estimated line from the reel then shot the fly forward to land in the trout's likely path. The next slurp was my black beetle disappearing. The commotion that erupted instantly lifted the heads of the other anglers. By now I was accepted and one shuffled to my side to assist with his landing net. "Want to keep it?" he questioned as the fish was lifted from the water.

"Not from here," I replied, Obviously delighted, my assistant bent to remove the hook. With the fish wrapped in the net and the line now slack the hook just dropped from its jaw. This allowed the release to be accomplished without delay.

"You were lucky to land him," offered my new friend. "He wasn't very well hooked."

"No barbs," I replied, "but they hold well until a fish is netted."

Being conservative people, anglers are difficult to convince about new or different ploys. In conversation they nod and apparently agree but rarely change their habits. I've talked frequently to fishermen about releasing fish and the ease with which the task can be done when barbless hooks are employed. Most release practically all the fish they catch yet most still use barbed hooks. Obviously talk is insufficient motivation. In contrast a simple demonstration has been all that was necessary to convince others.

In recent years I should have compiled some statistics comparing the holding capabilities of the fish hooked on barbed hooks with those on barbless hooks. But I haven't. I haven't because I cannot detect even the slightest difference. Any difference is in the mind only.

I can remember a recent rip to the Waiau River with Alan Pannett. In two days we hooked fifteen fish and landed fourteen. The fourteen landed were all with barbless hooks. The one we lost was on a barbed hook. Meaningless but somehow convincing. During that trip I was supposed to be showing Alan something and changing his ways. In fact, I think I learned as much if not more than he did. The most interesting point was that Alan termed 'premature release'. After hooking a fish and playing it for a time until it was under some control Alan allowed his line to become completely slack. Logically the barbless hook should have slipped from its hold and allowed the fish to go free. But even under these circumstances the hook held. Several times he tried to release trout prior to netting. Each time he failed. I've tried since and the result has been the same. Leaping rainbows hold, dogged browns hold — the only things that don't hold are inadvertently caught hats, coats or ears.

Telephone surveys throughout Auckland, Nelson and Invercargill have indicated that barbless hooks cannot be readily purchased in

New Zealand. Despite this inconvenience it takes little time or effort to remove the barbs from conventional hooks. In doing so there are a few points to remember. The job requires no sophisticated equipment — just a pair of pliers and perhaps a small file for the fastidious. The pliers should be flat on their gripping faces. The barb is removed by a gentle squeeze with the pliers. Take care to squeeze in one direction only (down onto the barb point) and do not squeeze too tightly. Two or three conservative squeezes may be better than one bold one. Twisting, turning and bending can remove the whole hook tip. The smaller the fly the more delicate the touch necessary. With size 16 and 18 I find my heavy pliers require only the slightest squeeze. Their weight in closing is almost sufficient to complete the flattening.

Barbs can be removed on the river bank but for anglers more organised than I, some preparations may be completed, probably more efficiently, using a tying vice (to hold the hook) at home.

The British made Partridge range of hooks is now available in New Zealand. Included in the very wide range available are barbless hooks. Currently, 'Tight Line,' of Waipukurau, mail order angling specialists stock the range. By the end of 1985 many sports stores will handle barbless hooks for the first time.

Use Of Forceps

Surgical forceps, or more correctly, artery forceps, assist an angler in removing hooks quickly. Obviously their delicate tips grip a hook more easily than large clumsy fingers. Their locking grip allows an almost infallible and very firm hold. With the hook so firmly gripped it is less necessary to grip the fish tightly, or at all, with barbless hooks and a net. Should a fish wriggle or jump once the hook is gripped it is an assistance to hook removal rather than a hindrance. If possible grip the curve of the hook rather than the body of the fly. The tight lock of forceps can damage fly dressings.

Photo 58
Artery forceps help remove hooks quickly.

Handling Fish

An angler who has netted a trout hooked with a barbless hook and who uses an efficient hook remover will find it necessary to handle fish to a very minimal degree. Often the netting will have entangled the catch sufficiently to hold it still and secure. Thus manipulation is restricted to the mouth area only. When the hook is removed the net can be used to place the fish back in the water. In this case too, if handling is required, the netting can be useful to grip the fish.

Ideals are not always possible. But remember, you are returning your catch for it to survive. Avoid handling the gill area. Do not squeeze the body cavity. A good place to grip a fish is just in front of the caudal (tail) fin. This strong muscle area is less vulnerable than the body cavity and head region. It was mentioned earlier that two anglers working together usually form a more efficient team in landing fish —

one hand gripping foward of the caudal fin and the other cupped under the front of the fish. The other angler, without the burden of an anxious trout, can concentrate on removing the hook.

Some Acclimatisation Society Officers avoid where possible handling trout with bare hands. A woollen mitten or sock provides a more efficient hold allowing a looser grip. A handkerchief will also do the same job. If it is necessary to slide one's hands along a trout's body while holding, always move them backwards, never forwards. Forward movement quickly lifts scales. Any sliding will take off some slime, one of a trout's protective layers.

An often overlooked factor in fish handling is that of temperature. Probably the most pleasant time to be catching trout is on a warm, sunny summer afternoon. That warm river bank is ideal for us but not for a trout. The shorter a fish's stay in the sun or on hot stones, the better.

Anglers Using Helicopters

I once had a friend whose wisdom I admired. I recall the time he talked about his uncle. "My uncle was a generous man," he said, "but at times his heart was in the wrong place. He was fond of his whisky and enjoyed a nip with anyone who called on him. He had two liquor cabinets, One contained the finest — Glenfiddich, Glenfarclas — the choicest pure malts that could purchased at the time. The second cabinet housed the local blends — the kind without the reputation or the price.

"When one of my uncle's friends would call, the blends were produced and enjoyed nonetheless, but when a new guest was introduced to the house, the finest appeared in somewhat pretentious hospitality. He could not see or maybe never thought that perhaps the people on whom he could rely, the ones he could trust, his real friends, the ones who belonged, should share the best."

In New Zealand we have some of the finest, choicest, purest trout fishing in the world. Like the best whisky its supply is not endless and it takes time to mature. Excess demands on it will reduce its maturing time and diminish its quality.

Yet we have in our country a growing number of guides who are quite happy to share our 'malt fishing' with strangers. Soon we will have to be content with the blends. The strangers are ferried into the remotest and best waters in helicopters in ever increasing numbers. They can afford it. We can't. An enigma in a supposedly egalitarian society.

Equally, if not more devastating, are some 'locals' who are literally pouring our malt down the drain. I spoke to one helicopter pilot two years ago who told me that he had ferried parties into the north-west Nelson area (and knew of others) for day trips. At the end of each day up to thirty trout had been killed (quite legally) and flown home. Another group, I learned, had enjoyed the Mokihinui River. They

Helicopter fishermen.

CRANTWINTER

landed plenty of fish which were housed behind a hut ready to be flown out the same day. Unfortunately the weather changed rapidly as it frequently does in the back country, and the helicopter could not fly in. By the time a flight was possible a heap of rotting fish lay at the rear of the hut — a thoughtless, useless waste.

The real problem with helicopter fishing is that it is largely carried out in rivers with delicate fish stocks. A few irresponsible people with no angling heart, using this transport can and do inflict immeasurable

146